The PACT Processes for
Performance-Based

Modular
Curriculum
Development

A Business Oriented Approach to
Curriculum Content Development
for an Enterprise Learning Context

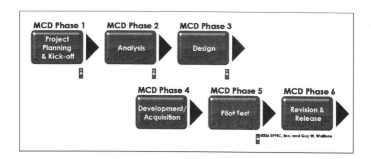

Guy W. Wallace

The Wallace 6-Pack
for Instructional Systems Design for an Enterprise Context
- Paperback and Kindle -

1. The Curriculum Manager's Handbook
2. Analysis of Performance Competence Requirements
3. Performance-Based Curriculum Architecture Design
4. Performance-Based Modular Curriculum Development
5. Developing Your Management Areas of Performance Competence
6. From Training to Performance Improvement Consulting

- Guy W. Wallace Books For Sale *new in 2011* -
See the Resources Tab at: www.eppic.biz

The PACT Processes for Performance-based Modular Curriculum Development

For additional copies of this book please go to the Resources Tab at:

www.eppic.biz

DEDICATION

To my wife Nancy – thank you for everything!

CONTENTS

3 levels of ISD Methodologies
with common Analysis and
Project Planning & Management Methodologies.

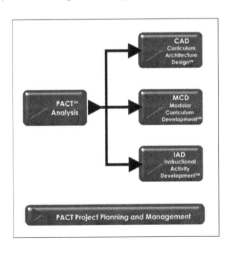

ACKNOWLEDGMENTS

The Origins of Modular Curriculum Development and the PACT Processes for T&D, Learning and Knowledge Management

The content of this book is based on more than 200 ISD – Instructional Systems Design applications I have been involved in since 1979.

My first Instructional Design effort using a Performance Model goes back to 1979. The first formal Modular Curriculum Development project using both the performance-based approach and the new Lesson Map format I created for a Group Process approach for design using a Design Team facilitated to process the analysis data, was in 1989/90 – for an audience of Supervisors at one of the Bell Operating Companies. The topic: Labor Relations.

I branded these methods as the PACT Processes for T&D, Learning and Knowledge Management.

Since my entry into the Instructional Design profession I have been involved in more than 50 formal MCD applications, mostly for Fortune 500 firms and mostly for their most critical Target Audiences in their most critical business processes. Most of my professional ISD life has been focused on CAD – Curriculum Architecture Design, where I have done over 70 projects for Clients since 1982.

MCD was intended to be the logical extension of those CAD methods into development, what is typically referred to as ADDIE – Analysis, Design, Development, Implementation and Evaluation. MCD was intended to leverage and pick up where the CAD analysis and design data left off – to speed that next part of the process.

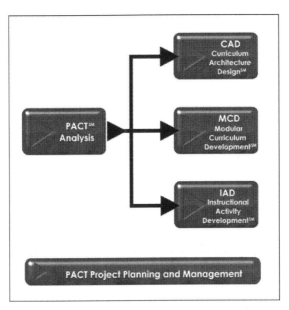

I have taught these methods to dozens of my staff members and hundreds of my Clients' staff, both formally and informally since 1984.

I have delivered presentations and development workshops both publically and privately on these PACT methods for

Project Planners/Managers, Analysts, CAD Designer and MCD Designer over 50 times since 1984.

This book is an updated, expanded excerpt from my 1999 book: lean-ISD.

Cover by Geary A. Rummler (in 1999)

This book has companion books, also new in 2011. They include "**Analysis of Performance Competence Requirements**" and, "**The PACT Processes for Performance-based Curriculum Architecture Design**."

Reviewers of lean-ISD from back in 1999…

Geary A. Rummler of the Performance Design Lab wrote:

"If you want to ground your fantasy of a 'corporate university' with the reality of a sound 'engineering' approach to instructional systems that will provide results, you should learn about the PACT Processes.

If you are the leader of, or a serious participant in, the design and implementation of a large-scale corporate curriculum, then this book is for you.

This system could be the difference between achieving bottom-line results with your training or being just another 'little red school house.' "

Note: The late Dr. Rummler was a mentor and friend going back to 1980. He redesigned (unasked) the cover for my lean-ISD book after spending two days with me reviewing it in great detail. I am forever grateful for what I learned from him in his writings, presentations and in-person.

Also in 1999 - Miki Lane, senior partner at MVM The Communications Group wrote a book review:

"*lean*-**ISD** takes all of the theory, books, courses, and pseudo job aids that are currently on the market about Instructional Systems Design and blows them out of the water.

Previous 'systems' approach books showed a lot of big boxes and diagrams, which were supposed to help the reader become proficient in the design process. Here is a book that actually includes all of the information that fell through the cracks of other ISD training materials and shows you the way to actually get from one step to another.

Guy adds all of the caveats and tips he has learned in more than 20 years of ISD practice and sprinkles them as job aids and stories throughout the book.

However, the most critical part of the book for me was that Guy included the project and people management elements of ISD in the book. Too often, ISD models and materials forget that we are working with real people in getting the work done. This book helps explain and illustrate best practices in ensuring success in ISD projects."

The PACT Processes are themselves a sub-set of a larger, umbrella set of Performance Improvement Methodologies that I have branded as EPPI – Enterprise Process Performance Improvement. Those EPPI methods also follow a similar process-orientation - as do these PACT Processes as covered in this book, and previously in lean-ISD. The goal is always the same, for the individual performers, for their function, and for the Enterprise.

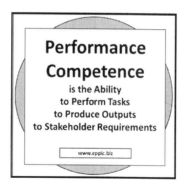

Guy W. Wallace

NOTE ON FORMATTING
FOR THIS BOOK

I have written this book deliberately for both a print format and for e-readers. Writing for e–readers as one key format necessitates using smaller, simple graphics – or avoiding them altogether. I have tended to avoid using my most complex graphics here. Readers may find relevant graphics for this book plus many additional resources on my Blog and elsewhere on my Web Site at:

www.eppic.biz

Search that site using the title of this book and the key words and phrases used in this book.

In the Event that that "cloud" dissipates someday, please search the Internet using the book's title and other key words and phrases that you find here.

I cannot promise that you'll find everything, but I will attempt to park that content in several places and in enough "clouds" to increase your probability in finding them.

The first publication of the analysis methodologies – using a Group Process – as presented in this book – was in:

The **November 1984 issue of The Performance & Instruction Journal** – of NSPI – now ISPI – the International Society for Performance Improvement.

My focus has always been on performance – which I now term: Performance Competence.

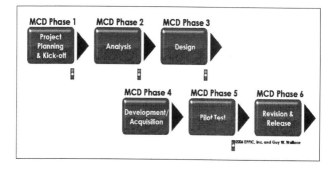

1 – WHAT IS MODULAR CURRICULUM DEVELOPMENT - MCD?

Chapter Overview

This chapter is intended to provide you with an introduction to this book, and to MCD – Modular Curriculum

Development – as both a set of Products and a set of
Processes – before covering these and other topics at a
greater depth in the succeeding chapters of this book.

Book Overview

This book presents an overview of MCD, and the details of
the processes and the practices so that you can begin to
adopt or adapt this approach to fit your situational needs and
constraints, and then begin practicing instructional design
using these proven methods.

MCD is similar to, but a little different from the traditional
ADDIE model, which is a project planning (process)
framework for the approach, and not a design tool that will
automatically create good instruction.

MCD Overview

MCD is an "instructional design" set of concept, models,
methods, tools and techniques for an Enterprise Learning
Context, as opposed to an Educational Learning Context or
a Personal Learning Context.

Like ADDIE, or SAT – Structured Approach to Training,
Modular Curriculum Development is a process, an approach
to instructional design (ID) or Instructional Systems Design
(ISD).

Modular Curriculum Development is an ISD model similar
to "ADDIE." MCD is the closest of the PACT Processes to
traditional ISD.

In the PACT Processes there are three levels of Instructional
Design. MCD sits in the mid-level between Curriculum

Architecture Design at the top, and Instructional Activity Development at the bottom. More on that later.

MCD differs a bit from ADDIE and other traditional ISD methods in its project structure, it's use of specific analysis and design templates, and its use of designated teams. As you'll read, even the phases in MCD are different than those in the A-D-D-I-E process.

The Modular Curriculum Development uses a Performance Model to define both ideal performance, and current gaps. Then that model of ideal performance is used to systematically derive the Knowledge and Skills that enable high performance. Then existing content can be assessed to determine its reuse potential.

This use of the Performance Model is key to ensuring that any T&D developed or reused is truly performance-based and therefor will have a positive impact on the Performance Competence of the Learners.

Again, MCD is one of three levels of design in the PACT Processes for Training, Learning and Knowledge Management.

Let's quickly review The PACT Processes and those 3 levels now.

The PACT Processes

PACT
PACT is an acronym – see this next graphic.

P erformance-based
A ccelerated
C ustomer-/Stakeholder-driven
T raining & Development℠

of any blend

©2002 EPPIC, Inc.
and Guy W. Wallace

The PACT Processes approach Enterprise Learning from the perspective of a shareholder or owner of the Enterprise. Check out the acronym again.

The three levels of ISD in the PACT Processes include:

- **CAD- Curriculum Architecture Design** – the modular design of performance-based instructional and informational content for Performance Competence development. This set of processes and practices produces a Learning/T&D Path and Planning Guide for On-Boarding and On-Going development needs – and helps your clients prioritize any of the existing gaps and maintenance needs.

- **MCD- Modular Curriculum Development** – this is the PACT Process' version of ADDIE: Analysis – Design – Development – Implementation – Evaluation – and is used to develop or buy and modify (as needed) one or several sets of Instructional Content or Events: either instruction and/or information needed at the moment of need, and/or before that moment of need.

- **IAD- Instructional Activity Development** – is also a PACT Process' version of ADDIE: Analysis – Design – Development – Implementation – Evaluation – however this is used to develop one or several components of a typical package of Instructional Content a.k.a.: Events - such as Knowledge Tests, Performance Tests, Case Studies, Performance Demonstrations, Examples, etc. This methodology-set is used when the client needs/wants pieces of Instruction – with the intent to "maybe" later wrap these first pieces with additional content to create a more holistic piece of instruction.

These three levels of ISD are enabled by common **Analysis** and common **Project Planning & Management concept, models, methods, tools and techniques**.

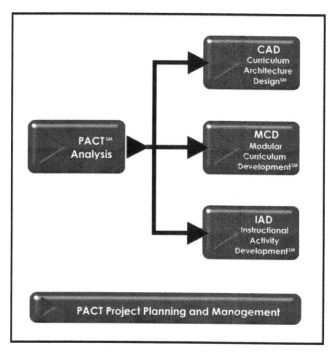

PACT is…

Performance-based

At the heart of the PACT Processes are the analytic methods to build models of performance and analyze the Knowledge and Skills on which performance is based.

The Performance Models capture both ideal and actual performance (a gap analysis from that ideal), and then facilitate the systematic derivation of enabling Knowledge and Skills. During the design process, Performance Models are used to ensure that T&D content focuses on performance first.

The Performance Model data establishes performance objectives as the terminal learning objectives – immediately establishing the evaluation specifications for what's generally referred to as Level 2 and Level 3 measures.

Accelerated

For almost three decades, the PACT Processes and the methods, tools and techniques have been refined through more than 200 ISD projects addressing more than 200 types of jobs, conducted by this author alone. My business partners, staff and the staff of my Clients have proven these methods, winning awards at times, on hundreds and hundreds of additional projects.

The goal, driven by the Client needs, was always to do these projects *quickly!* But the project work products also had to be of high quality.

To help accelerate the project and ensure good results, PACT Processes all use a highly structured (but flexible) series of processes, practices and templates. The templates include plans, guides, job aids/models, and database tools.

No project needs to start from scratch and invent the process, practices, tools or outputs.

The PACT Processes and templates provide a starting point upon which each project can be custom-designed as needed, if needed, to meet the Client's situational needs.

Customer-/Stakeholder-driven

T&D like other purchased products or services, either *adds value* for Stakeholders by contributing to the bottom line, or it does not.

The PACT Processes intentionally focus on the business side of T&D and re-empower and facilitate the Customer and Stakeholders in making all of the **business decisions** typical of an ISD effort.

The Customer-/Stakeholder-driven orientation goes further than collaboration – it enables them to drive the processes and practices of ISD for their own benefit. After all – they live with the consequences for those decisions.

Bringing the Customer orientation into the PACT Processes produces T&D products that are:

- Developed with input and insight from the users - the team approach inherent in the PACT Processes uses Customer participation and ownership, leading to increased support and resources
- Bench-tested and field-tested prior to widespread deployment - reviews and pilot testing are part of the PACT Processes
- Marketed like any other product - for example, with catalogs and brochures
- Designed to accommodate continuous change and thus minimize future costs over the entire product life cycle - via the use of components, "modular"

content of training – and not a collection of modules

This Customer orientation directly benefits ISD Customers and the Enterprise as a whole.

MCD and CAD

Modular Curriculum Development (MCD) is a *lean*-**ISD** methodology for the development of T&D specified by a Curriculum Architecture Design effort; or it may stand alone without a prior CAD effort. That is by design.

One does not need to conduct a CAD to develop any L&D. One could start with a key Event or two, or start a CAD effort with those already in place, and then do a CAD to complete the effort.

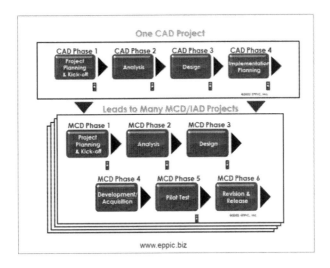

www.eppic.biz

IAD – Instructional Activity Development

IAD is a subset of MCD.

It is used instead of an MCD effort when your Client needs the component pieces of Instruction – and not the entire instructional package, such as a T&D or L&D product, be that a course, a workshop, a seminar, an e-learning module, a webinar or a Structured OJT package.

Perhaps all your Client needs and wants right now are Performance Tests, or Application Exercises, or a group of Product Demonstrations, or overviews or details about some topic – and perhaps later they might want to "wrap" those component pieces, produced first, with other content to create a more traditional set of Instruction.

Perhaps they have a big Sales meeting coming up and they need these component pieces for that – and they might want to create the full blown set of T&D products later. That has been my experience.

Or perhaps they wish to develop Performance Tests for use in a Pay Progression Program – and not use written tests – but use actual performance as required on the job. That is also an application where this has been used from my project experiences.

IAD gives the ISD Customers that flexibility – and gives the ISD Suppliers a way to do IAD now - and perhaps do MCD later, more smoothly – and more efficiently and effectively – as needed/desired by their Client. Think: let's design and develop all of the radios and music/audio players for cars – and develop the cars later, maybe. Let's make sure that everything will integrate smoothly will zero rework of the radios/players.

CAD-MCD-IAD

The purpose of the Curriculum Architecture Design process is to *design* an overall curriculum architecture. The purpose of the Modular Curriculum Development (MCD) process is to *develop* T&D Events from a prior Curriculum Architecture Design, or without it having been done previously. And the IAD process is to build component pieces for supporting some aspects of the entire job – or more narrowly focused aspect of the job.

If a CAD does precede the MCD or IAD processes, the macro-level analysis and design work from the CAD is used during the MCD/IAD processes to jump start those efforts and take them to a micro, more detailed level. During MCD/IAD, teams continue to refine the CAD design data, sticking to the overall CAD macro design to insure that all of the content pieces work in harmony to develop Performance Competence.

If a Curriculum Architecture Design does not precede the MCD/IAD process, then the teams spend the time needed specifying the detailed analysis data and then developing the detailed designs for T&D Lessons and Events.

Back to MCD - and IAD – as IAD is a sub-set of MCD.

MCD Outputs

Outputs/products of the Modular Curriculum Development process include those from analysis, design, and development activities.

These analysis outputs are the same as those produced by a CAD effort and include:

- Target Audience data
- Performance Models data
- Knowledge/Skill Matrices data
- Existing T&D Assessments data

Modular Curriculum Development's instructional design outputs are at three levels – to feed development - and include:

- Event Specs and Maps
- Lesson Specs and Maps
- Instructional Activity Specs

Note: a Spec is an output with more words than visuals; while a Map is more visual than wordy, but includes words.

They often go together – for the top 2 levels, but for some items (Instructional Activity Specs) I do not include the "Map" as I thought it was simply not necessary.

You may need to adapt that philosophy and approach regarding Maps and Specs as your needs dictate.

If a Curriculum Architecture Design precedes a Modular Curriculum Development effort, the Event Specs and Module Specs will have already been developed; and those Modules of the CAD will be converted to Lessons. More on that later.

Depending on the delivery platforms, the media and mode of instruction and/or information, the Modular Curriculum Development efforts (and in IAD efforts) the Development phase's outputs include:

- T&D and supporting materials for Pilot-Testing, such as
    - Facilitator guides and materials
    - Participant guides
    - Administrator guides

These can be for deployment/access of such media and modes as:

- Instructor-led courses
- E-Learning content
- Webinar content
- Structured OJT (mentor and coaches and learner materials) content
- Etc.

Also, these other outputs might be included in what an MCD or IAD effort might produce:

- Pilot-Test brochures
- Other communications and marketing materials

MCD Processes

Modular Curriculum Development (MCD) projects *produce* modular T&D – Training & Development products – or if you prefer: modular L&D – Learning & Development products.

The gated PACT Process model for Modular Curriculum Development is shown in the following graphic.

Note that the 6 phases have only been "wrapped" into two lines for fitting onto the pages of this book.

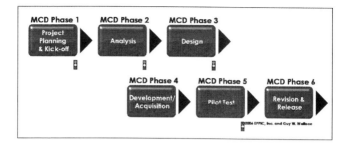

Note: the six phases can be combined as needed.

The 6 phases would more typically be shown as a straight line, a linear line – as the PACT Process for MCD is not an iterative approach – where one bounces back and forth from one phase to another to eventually get it right. MCD, as well as CAD and IAD don't iterate at the phase level – as that would then not be predictable in terms of schedules and costs.

What is done, in place of such iteration - is successive levels of data analysis or design and articulation, phase by phase.

After collecting macro-data and getting that **approved**, the next phase or phases penetrate deeper into that data and flesh it out further, in successive approximations to finally arrive at the details needed - for the next phase and its steps in the process.

Using a method that does Analysis, then Design, then Development – only to bounce back to Analysis after figuring out that something got missed in the earlier attempt at Analysis is anathema to The PACT Processes. That potential has been engineered out.

In PACT one does not bounce back and forth – one dives in deeper after a review and approval/modification process and further details the design with what some might call additional analysis data. Otherwise all predictability for schedule, touch-time and cycle-time is lost – and that is not a good business practice, and is not good stewardship of shareholder equity.

MCD and IAD

Again, Instructional Activity Development (IAD) is the micro-level PACT Process in which certain *components* of T&D are developed. IAD is a sub-set of MCD in that way.

For example, an IAD project may produce instructional activities such as knowledge tests, Performance Tests, simulation exercises, and performance aids. These are also produced in the MCD efforts.

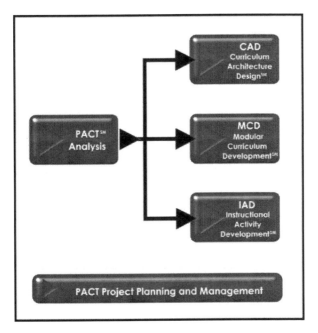

The gated PACT Process Model for Instructional Activity Development is the same as for MCD – the 6 phase model.

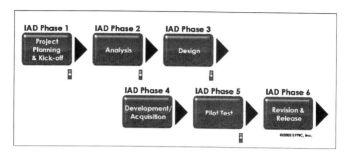

While the IAD flow is similar to Modular Curriculum Development, the two processes produce different, but overlapping levels of instructional components.

Again, MCD typically produces events or courses, while IAD produces activities that may become part of events or courses or stand on their own. This provides flexibility for the ISD Customers. They can have pieces of instruction sooner, and wrap those in an instructional package later – if that is what they need and want. Or perhaps having those piece-parts – placed in a wiki – is all that they'll ever need or want.

The PACT Processes for MCD and IAD use a team approach to conduct most activities. This is done to reduce overall cycle time by getting the right data the first time, reducing rework for analysis, design and development, which reduces costs and cycle time.

The PACT Processes *can* be conducted using the more traditional approach of separate, individual interviews; however, this increases cycle times and costs.

The key teams involved in the PACT Processes for IAD still
include, just as an MCD effort includes:

- Project Steering Team
- Analysis Team
- Design Team
- Development Team
- Pilot-Test Team
- ISD Team

The MCD/IAD Project Steering Team is most critical to the
overall success. Members of this team oversee the entire
project. They also handpick Analysis Team members.

At some point in the ISD Customer and ISD Supplier
relationship the Project Steering Team – or an Advisory
Council – may forgo the formal management of project
efforts and the Customer/Stakeholders may empower the
ISD Suppliers to go on without their active involvement.

This is a double edged sword.

Without the active guidance and support of the Customer
and Stakeholders – the efforts may not get the attention they
need – the business decisions made properly - or the
resources needed.

On the other hand, developing the next batch of Product
Knowledge content after the first 25 does not need the same
level of guidance – but it may still require the same level of
support – support from within the Customer's and other
Stakeholders' organizations. From their people.

The MCD/IAD Analysis Team conducts the various types
of analyses required in a PACT project. The Analysis Team
is typically composed of Master Performers and Subject
Matter Experts who work with the ISD Project Manager and

other ISD professionals. The Analysis Team might also include managers or supervisors of the target audiences along with novice performers, as appropriate to the effort.

The Design Team is a subset of the Analysis Team. It provides input for the design of whichever components are appropriate for the particular PACT Process - a design of the Curriculum Architecture, a design of modular Events (courses), or a design of Instructional Activities such as Performance Tests.

The ISD Team includes the ISD professionals who plan and manage the project, conduct and facilitate the analysis, design, development and pilot-test efforts, and participate in all other work necessary to move the project forward to completion.

MCD/IAD teams are covered in detail later in this book in chapters 13 and 14.

From here on out this book will consider IAD as a sub-set of MCD and will stop referring to it as a separate methodology. If you can do MCD efforts – you can do IAD efforts.

Chapter Summary & Transition

This chapter was intended to provide you with an introduction to this book, and to MCD – Modular Curriculum Development – as both a set of Products and a set of Processes.

Key characteristics of the Modular Curriculum Development process affect the business or the organizations using the process. Teaming is critical – for getting the right data the first time at the right time in the process.

Putting in place the tools and templates necessary, as well as using the proven processes and practices, will be critical. These will be covered throughout this book

The MCD process is

- Structured – MCD phases, tasks, and templates expedite the development effort in a proven, standardized way.
- Gated – The use of Project Steering Teams and Gate Review Meetings ensures that only projects with positive effects on the business are carried out and that project issues are discussed as they arise.
- In control – The Project Manager and steering team have good visibility of the overall process and of the work products developed during the project.

Modular Curriculum Development helps ensure that the organization financial resources are allocated and invested in instruction and/or information needed in the moment of need/ and/or prior to that moment of need. Those are decision that are more business decisions than instructional design decisions.

The MCD methods produce performance impacting content – content that develops Performance Competence.

In addition, the Modular Curriculum Development process is flexible. Its six phases can be combined as needed. It allows for either the development or acquisition of authentic enough T&D content — whichever "means" has more benefits to the organization – in terms of performance impact at lower costs and cycle times.

This chapter flows logically into the next, however your needs may cause you to want to skip around.

The following are the chapter titles and page numbers to assist you with your personal navigation needs.

Suggested Chapter Reflection & Reaction

I would suggest that prior to jumping into whichever chapter meets your needs that you give pause for a moment to reflect on the following and make some notes:

- Does this have applicability for me?

- What can I adopt from what I have read here?

- What are my potential needs for adaptation?

- What other issues do I see that I will need to address before embracing?

Please make note of your thoughts before proceeding.

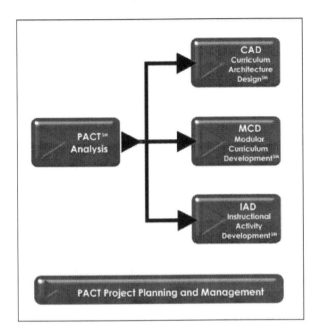

3 levels of ISD Methodologies
with common Analysis and
Project Planning & Management Methodologies.

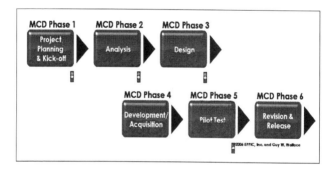

2 – MCD BENEFITS FOR THE CUSTOMERS OF ISD – INSTRUCTIONAL SYSTEMS DESIGN

Chapter Overview

This chapter is intended to provide you with an overview and details of why your ISD Customers might want you, their ISD Supplier, to use these methods.

WIIFT – what's in it for them?

You need to understand that. WIIFY – what's in it for you, besides what's in it for your Customers, is the topic of the next chapter in this book, chapter 3.

Now – WIIFT.

What's In It For Your Customers?

The process structure built into the Modular Curriculum Development methodology engages the right Stakeholders to obtain the right input and make the right decisions at the right time.

The MCD process structure and the practices, especially the use of teams and templates, shortens the project time cycle and reduces costs for T&D projects.

Their use also increases the quality of the T&D products and services produced, by focusing on desired terminal performance as the basis for developing T&D. They focus on the Performance Competence Requirements.

Performance Competence
is the Ability
to Perform Tasks
to Produce Outputs
to Stakeholder Requirements

www.eppic.biz

If your instructional content is not geared to enable
Performance Competence – then it is a poor use of
shareholder equity.

The structured MCD design processes allocate T&D content
into more shareable chunks, thereby reducing future, life
cycle costs.

Sharable in MCD means either "as is" or "after
modification." And "after modification" means derivatives –
and the need to name, number, store and track those
derivatives – with the benefit of more authenticity for the
Learner – and greater impact for the Customer – the
Learner's management.

The Client Gate Review Meetings in the Modular
Curriculum Development process phases provide a way for
project participants to work together "for the Clients" in an
accelerated manner, to produce performance-based T&D.

ISD professionals retain control of most ISD decisions;
while Clients, the Customers and Stakeholders in the T&D
marketplace, gain control of all of the business decisions
inherent in any T&D project. The Gate Review Meetings
and processes ensure that T&D Customers and Stakeholders
are systematically engaged for collective success — a
collaborative win-win for all.

The use of teams also helps to get the right people involved
at the right time and for the right reasons. Teams provide for
increased participation in project activities and increased
ownership of project results – good for both ISD Customers
and ISD Suppliers.

Modular Curriculum Development benefits accrue to T&D
Customers and Suppliers alike. The key ISD Customer
benefits are ownership of the content and lean participation
in the process. Customers gain control over the destiny of

their T&D content – and over their ISD Supplier – and over the consequences of adequate instruction – or not.

This is a business relationship.

The MCD processes have appropriate forums to discuss the right issues at the right time.

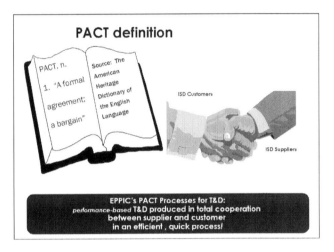

The MCD T&D content is focused squarely on performance and is built by benchmarking the best performance of the Customer's Master Performers from within the Customer's own organizations. Or from outside if there are no Master Performers. Or from the best guesses of experts when the effort is a totally new, a "greenfield" effort.

Let's look closer but quick at the analysis data that the Analysis Team of Master Performers and others produce, with the help of their ISD Supplier's staff who facilitate the analysis processes.

Performance Model Data

This data includes:

- Areas of Performance (AoPs)
- Outputs per AoP
- Measures and Standards per Output
- Tasks per Output
- Roles/Responsibilities per Task
- Typical gaps when Outputs don't meet Measures and Standards
- Potential Causes per Gap

AoPs are like the separate activity blocks of ADDIE - or of Six Sigma's DMAIC.

ADDIE...

- Analysis
- Design
- Development
- Implementation
- Evaluation

DMAIC...

- Define
- Measure
- Analyze
- Improve
- Control

Those were examples of the Areas of Performance. For each the Outputs, etc. would be gathered in the analysis process.

These MCD analysis data will be covered more extensively in chapter 7.

This data has many other benefits for the Customers; those will be presented in chapter 16.

Enabling K/S Data

This data includes:

- Knowledge/Skill items per the 17 K/S categories - or some sub-set of those categories
- Assessments of:
    - o Criticality to Performance Competence
    - o Difficulty to Learn
    - o Volatility of the Content
    - o Depth Needed (awareness, knowledge, skill)

These data have uses in both uncovering reuse potential of existing content – and specifying new content for build or buy actions; as well as feeding other HR-type systems, such as performance assessment, development planning and others – see below.

These will also be covered more extensively in chapters 7 and 16.

Other Uses of the Data

The Customers' uses for these sets of data, other than for the CAD effort itself, include:

- Process/Performance troubleshooting
- Job Design and Organization Design
- Staff Planning systems
- Career Planning systems

- Recruiting and Selection systems
- Job Descriptions
- Performance Appraisal systems
- Pay Progression systems

I have been involved in at least one if not dozens of each of these types of "other uses" since the early 1980s; and my business partners and my staff over the years have been involved in many more of these specific applications. Even my Customers' staff, trained formally or informally by me have done these.

A book that I and my two business partners published in 1994, The Quality Road Map, framed this data as part of a Business Architecture, and described many of these types of efforts to improve overall Quality of an Enterprise. See the reference to this book in chapter 18.

These "other uses" for the analysis data are covered more extensively in chapter 16.

Features, Benefits, and Possible Advantages Specifically for Customers

The features, benefits, and possible advantages specifically for the Customers for conducting an MCD effort and using the data perhaps for "other uses" follow.

The Features
The key features for the Customer for this approach to upfront design of a curriculum and for the data generated includes:

- The modular T&D/L&D Events are performance-oriented, reflecting the needs for ideal performance as articulated and conceded to by the handpicked Master Performers and other Subject Matter Experts involved in both the Analysis and Design efforts.

- The analysis data is created and owned by the ISD Customer, not by the ISD Supplier

- The analysis data is organized in a logical manner and enables more effective and efficient change management of the data and final instructional products

The Benefits

The key benefits for the Customer for this approach to upfront design of a curriculum and for the data generated includes:

- The MCD methodology creates a collaboration between ISD Suppliers and Customers that puts the Customers in the driver's seat when it comes to the key business decisions inherent in every ISD effort.

- The ISD Customer has the final say in terms of what L&D *could be*, *should be* and *will be*. The ROI rationale for doing any or all of it is up to the Customer who lives with the consequences for those decisions.

- The analysis data is easier to keep up to date by the Customer – and forecast changes needed to the curricula – reducing cycle times and costs

The Advantages

The key Advantages for the Customer for approach to upfront design of a curriculum and for the data generated include:

- Instructional content is all geared toward the specific Performance Competence required for that job or sets of jobs, and is not based on or is in support of generic Competencies.

    o Ask yourself – if you hired everyone who already had the list of Competencies that your Enterprise uses, or that you have seen, would they actually be able to do the jobs as required without any additional instruction or guidance?

    No, usually they probably would not. Those are most often enablers of performance, not the performance that is needed.

- The analysis and design methods are quicker than traditional approaches and produce data that is better, developed fast and cheaper than other methods

- The ISD Customer has the final say in terms of what L&D *could be, should be* and *will be*. The ROI rationale for doing any or all of it is up to the Customers, who live with the consequences for those decisions. Just as you are responsible for the gas mileage of the car that you choose to buy after you've made the purchase, not the manufacturer or salesperson.

- Tying many of the other HR-related systems together with this data to help them work more seamlessly toward the goals of enabling the Customers' Process requirements via people who are Performance Competent.

Again, these other uses for the data will be covered in chapter 16.

Chapter Summary & Transition

This chapter was intended to you with an overview and details of why your ISD Customers might want you their ISD Supplier to use these methods. WIIFT – what's in it for them?

There are many business benefits to be derived from the PACT Processes for T&D. The benefits help shareholders, Customers, ISD staff, and ISD suppliers and vendors.

The key benefits are best summarized as follows.

- Improved T&D quality and effectiveness due to its focus on human performance requirements within business processes
- Reduced T&D life-cycle costs due to modular design and the ability to use predefined tools and templates during analysis and design
- Reduced cycle time due to the use of predefined roles and responsibilities, tasks, inputs, and outputs

These benefits produce improvements in T&D quality, delivery time, and cost—better, faster, cheaper. But bottom line – it's all about the Performance Competence of the Target Audiences.

The PACT Processes for T&D provide a proactive, strategic, *lean*-**ISD** approach to the development and deployment of performance-based T&D interventions.

PACT's orientation to Customer processes and to the business itself make the PACT Processes appropriate for use in today's business climate, where continuous re-engineering and improvement efforts depend on critical T&D products to help earn the anticipated return on those investments.

As you learn about the features of the PACT Processes in more detail, other benefits will become apparent.

This chapter flows logically into the next, however your needs may cause you to want to skip around.

The following are the chapter titles and page numbers to assist you with your personal navigation needs.

Suggested Chapter Reflection & Reaction

I would suggest that prior to jumping into whichever chapter meets your needs that you give pause for a moment to reflect on the following and make some notes:

- Does this have applicability for me?

- What can I adopt from what I have read here?

- What are my potential needs for adaptation?

- What other issues do I see that I will need to address before embracing?

Please make note of your thoughts before proceeding.

Guy W. Wallace

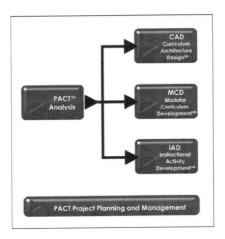

3 levels of ISD Methodologies
with common Analysis and
Project Planning & Management Methodologies.

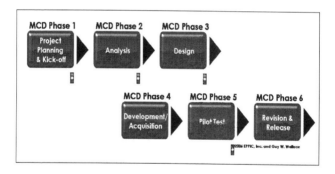

3 - MCD BENEFITS FOR THE SUPPLIERS OF ISD – INSTRUCTIONAL SYSTEMS DESIGN

Chapter Overview

This chapter is intended to provide you with an overview and details of why you, as an ISD Supplier, might want use these methods.

WIIFY – what's in it for you?

We'll describe the major Outputs of the MCD effort including those covered in the last chapter, as all of those that were of particular benefit for ISD Customers are also of benefit to ISD Suppliers; and then we'll cover the features, benefits, and possible advantages of this approach and the data generated specifically for the ISD Suppliers.

It would be best if you had read that last chapter before this one.

WIIFY?

The key benefits to the ISD Supplier have to do with being in the driver's seat for Instructional Design decisions, while leaving the business decisions inherent in all ISD effort to the ISD Customers, who live with the consequences of both those decisions and the effectiveness of the ISD work done by their ISD Suppliers (you).

Let's begin with the benefits derived from the Outputs.

Benefits of the MCD Effort Outputs for the ISD Suppliers

The key additional outputs of an MCD effort , beyond those covered in the last chapter, that are of benefit to the Suppliers of ISD efforts include the creation of the following:

- Project Plan
- Target Audience data
- Existing T&D (L&D) Assessments

- Event Specs
- Lesson Specs
- 5-Tier Content Inventory
- Implementation Plan

Let's overview each set of outputs phase by phase.

Phase 1: Project Planning & Kick-Off
The MCD effort produces one major output in the first phase:

- A Project Plan

This creates a pact, an agreement/contract between the PACT Processes Customers and Suppliers. This output lays out for both Customers and Suppliers, who will do what and when. Both the cycle time of efforts and the burden time are forecasted.

This will be covered more extensively in chapter 6.

Phase 2: Analysis
The MCD effort produces four types of analysis data in the second phase:

- Target Audience data
- Performance Model data
- Enabling Knowledge/Skill data
- Existing T&D (L&D) Assessments data

The Performance Model and the K/S data were overviewed in the last chapter. These define both the terminal performance objectives – leading directly to the terminal learning objectives and the evaluation measures for Levels 2 and 3: mastery and transfer, respectively.

The Target Audience data provides an agreed upon focus as to which target audiences will be served fully, partially, or not at all in the project efforts. This output is of particular utility to the ISD Suppliers in that it describes whose needs are to be met. I like to list all of the:

- Primary Target Audiences
- Secondary Target Audiences
- Tertiary Target Audiences

Primary Target Audiences are those audiences for whom we intend to get all of their performance and needs identified and addressed on the Paths. They are in the box!

Secondary Target Audiences are those audiences where we might identify some of their needs – and we may or may not need to design Paths for them. The Project Steering Team decides that as part of the project scoping effort. They sit borderline on the edge of our box.

Tertiary Target Audiences are those that some might think we will address, but are not part of our targets. I've found it best – decades ago – to list them as "not to be addressed" and to review this list with the Project Steering over and over again – to get it clarified with everyone. They are outside of our box! Note: I have been burned on this more than once, and so I have learned to repeat this often.

Once the Project Steering Teams is clear amongst themselves – an issue at times – as to who is "in the box" or not, we are good-to-go into the Analysis Phase and begin by getting the data needed on these Target Audiences and their Performance Competence requirements and enablers.

The assessment of Existing T&D content will insure that content is reused, as appropriate, either "as is" or "after modification" – to insure that it is authentic enough to have an impact back on the job for the Learners. This output is of particular utility to the ISD Suppliers in that it help them see what is reusable "as is" and "after medication" and what from the inventory of existing content is "not reusable" at all, for this effort.

These will also be covered more extensively in chapter 7.

Phase 3: Design

The MCD effort produces three major outputs, three levels of design in the design phase:

- The Event-level Specifications - an Event is a.k.a.: Course, Workshop, Session, etc. - and an Event Map
- The Lesson-level Specifications and Lesson Maps
- The Instructional Activity Specifications

Event Specs and Maps define the Events – and their makeup of Lessons – unless these came from an earlier CAD – Curriculum Architecture Design effort – then these would be at a Module level needing to be converted into Lessons.

In thinking about the Events, and their Lessons and their Instructional Activities – think: map of a country, the states, and the counties (or the equivalent in your country). Zooming in and out of these three levels is what the MCD design outputs enable.

These outputs are of particular utility to the ISD Suppliers in that it provides guidance later in the post-MCD Design phase for guiding the development by the developers.

Lesson Specs and Maps define the Lessons – and list the one or more Events that they go into. In complex MCD efforts one Lesson might go into several Events – if there is more than one Event being designed in the one MCD effort.

The 5-Tier Module Inventory, part of the Infrastructure to be covered in chapter 12, is of particular utility to the ISD Suppliers in that it provides guidance for storage and searching for existing content that might be available for reuse.

These three design outputs will be covered more extensively in chapter 8.

Phase 4: Development

And in the fourth phase of an MCD effort the teams produce:

- The Pilot-Test versions of the T&D (L&D) Event(s) – including the Lessons and the Instructional Activities of the Lessons

These outputs are unique to the media/mode for the Instruction and Information intended and specified by the design outputs.

These will also be covered more extensively in chapter 9.

Phase 5: Pilot-Test

And in the fifth phase an MCD effort produces:

- Pilot-Test Results
- Revision Recommendations
- Revision Specifications

The Clients of the Project Steering Team review the results of the Pilot-test and the ISD Supplier's Revision Recommendations. Whatever is agreed to then become the Revision Specifications - and those are used in the final phase of an MCD effort.

These will be covered more extensively in chapter 10.

Phase 6: Revision & Release
And in the sixth phase an MCD effort produces:

- Final materials – appropriate to the media/model for the intended Instruction and/or Information

These outputs are unique to the media/model for the Instruction and information.

These materials are "released" into the systems for on-going deployment and/or access.

These will also be covered more extensively in chapter 11.

Features, Benefits, and Possible Advantages Specifically for the ISD Suppliers

The features, benefits, and possible advantages specifically for the Suppliers for conducting an MCD effort and using the data for "other uses" follow.

The Features

The key features for the Suppliers for this approach to upfront design of performance-based Content, instructional and/or informational, and for other data generated includes:

- Collaboration with the Client (Customers and Stakeholders) where they are in the driver's seat for all business decisions and also providing a forum for the ISD Suppliers to make their case from a "science of learning" perspective – to avoid cognitive overload and all sorts of other issues typically faced later by Clients who wanted it all learned under impossible conditions that they themselves typically imposed.

- The Analysis data from the Performance Models and Enabling K/S Matrices provide inputs from the very beginning for the definition and construction of the evaluation of transfer and mastery and for the articulation of two levels of learning objectives:
  - o Terminal learning objectives
  - o Enabling learning objectives.

- The analysis data is created and owned by the ISD Customer, not by the ISD Supplier, who facilitates its creation using the voices of the Master Performers – and others – who were handpicked by the Project Steering Team.

The Benefits

The key benefits for the ISD Supplier for this approach to upfront design of a curriculum and for the data generated includes:

- The MCD methodology creates a collaboration between ISD Suppliers and ISD Customers that puts the Customers in the driver's seat when it comes to the key business decisions inherent in every ISD effort.

- The ISD Customer has the final say in terms of what L&D *could be, should be* and *will be.* The ROI rationale for doing any or all of it is up to the Customer who lives with the consequences for those decisions. The ISD Suppliers don't get stuck with what is sometimes "no-win" decision making.

- The analysis data is organized in a logical manner and leads to a better approach for Change Management of content – as all content links back to the analysis data – and is therefore easier to work with Clients to forecast, track – before or as they hit – and then manage the change processes.

- The modular T&D/L&D Events are performance-oriented, reflecting the needs for ideal performance as articulated and conceded to by the handpicked Master Performers and other Subject Matter Experts involved in the Analysis and design efforts.

The Advantages

The key Advantages for the ISD Supplier for this approach to the upfront design of a curriculum and for the data generated includes:

- Instructional content is all geared toward specific Performance Competence required for that job, and is not based on generic competencies.

- The analysis and design methods produce data that is better, developed faster and cheaper than with other ISD methods.

- The ISD Customer has the final say in terms of what L&D *could be*, *should be* and *will be*. The ROI rationale for doing any or all of it is up to the Customers who live with the consequences for those decisions.

- Tying all of the other HR-related systems together helps the ISD Supplier work more seamlessly toward the goals of enabling the Customers' Process by providing Content to develop people who are Performance Competent.

Chapter Summary & Transition

This chapter was intended to provide you with an overview and details of why you, as an ISD Supplier, might want use these MCD methods. WIIFY – what's in it for you?

The key benefits are best summarized, just as they were in the previous chapter, as follows.

- Improved T&D quality and effectiveness due to its focus on human performance requirements within business processes
- Reduced T&D life-cycle costs due to modular design and the ability to use predefined tools and templates during analysis and design
- Reduced cycle time due to the use of predefined roles and responsibilities, tasks, inputs, and outputs

These benefits produce improvements in T&D quality, delivery time, and cost—better, faster, cheaper.

The PACT Processes for T&D provide a proactive, strategic, *lean*-**ISD** approach to the development and deployment of performance-based T&D interventions.

This chapter flows logically into the next, however your needs may cause you to want to skip around.

The following are the chapter titles and page numbers to assist you with your personal navigation needs.

Suggested Chapter Reflection & Reaction

I would suggest that prior to jumping into whichever chapter meets your needs that you give pause for a moment to reflect on the following and make some notes:

- Does this have applicability for me?

- What can I adopt from what I have read here?

- What are my potential needs for adaptation?

- What other issues do I see that I will need to address before embracing?

Please make note of your thoughts before proceeding.

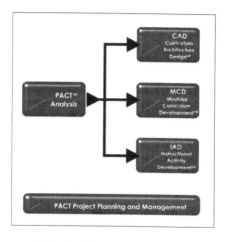

3 levels of ISD Methodologies
with common Analysis and
Project Planning & Management Methodologies.

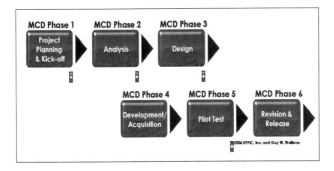

4 – MCD BENEFITS FOR THE ENTERPRISE STAKEHOLDERS

Chapter Overview

This chapter is intended to provide you with the key benefits for the Enterprise for conducting Modular Curriculum

Development projects for their most critical Target Audiences.

This will focus on the ROI achieved through 7 key benefits.

I will also provide you with 3 Case Studies and one Testimonial.

As we have just covered all of the key outputs of an MCD effort in the previous two chapters, here we'll just stick to the benefits and to the ROI potential. And I'll provide some real-world Case Studies and a Testimonial from clients who experienced these methods.

Let's begin.

Benefits for the Enterprise

This next graphic sums up the reasons for doing MCD – Modular Curriculum Development efforts. There are seven key benefits that are possible from starting your development efforts with Curriculum Architecture design.

1. Increased	**Performance Impact**
2. Increased	**Modular Design Reuse**
3. Reduced	**Development time and costs**
4. Reduced	**Inventory Systems costs**
5. Reduced	**Administrative Systems costs**
6. Reduced	**Deployment Systems costs**
7. Reduced	**Maintenance Systems costs**

Modular Curriculum Development methods and leverage appropriate reuse possibilities – at a level below the "lesson level" as the "learning object" approach typically does. If you only share at that level, and not lower, you may not get more than the first of these seven benefits using the MCD approach.

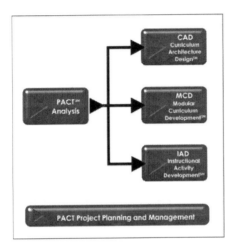

You'll get that performance orientation due to the MCD effort's use of the Performance Model, when you capture what Performance Competence is required for the Target Audiences.

You can get content reuse easily enough using other ISD methodologies – but unless it's appropriate reuse – that reuse can lead to wasted time and effort – and the money that that represents for everyone involved in those L&D Events. And that's not good stewardship of Shareholder equity.

Reuse of content that isn't authentic enough – won't lead to learning or Performance Competence.

Let's review the seven benefits and how they come about.

Benefit 1: Increased Performance Impact

This benefit is derived from using the Performance Model to first capture and articulate the Performance Competence Requirements of the Target Audience – and then systematically deriving the enabling Knowledge/Skills from that data. Those two analysis data outputs drive all of that performance orientation into the Lessons and Events.

Benefit 2: Increased Modular Design Reuse

This benefit is due to the predisposition in PACT in both the CAD and the MCD methods to look for existing content after the Performance Models and Enabling K/S Matrices are developed – and using that analysis data as the shopping criteria for assessing all Instruction and Information relevant to the needs captured in those Performance Models and Enabling K/S Matrices.

Benefit 3: Reduced Development Time and Costs

This benefit is derived from both the structured approach of the PACT processes and its use of teams of the right expertise, and for the various templates and methods.

Plus the design process avoids unnecessary duplicative content – due to the final analysis step of assessing all Instruction and Information relevant to the needs captured in those Performance Models and Enabling K/S Matrices – and watching out for inadvertent redundancies during the design efforts.

Benefit 4: Reduced Inventory System Costs

This benefit is due to avoiding unnecessary duplicative content in the Design phase's steps.

Benefit 5: Reduced Administrative Systems Costs
This benefit is due to avoiding unnecessary duplicative content in the Design phase's steps.

Benefit 6: Reduced Deployment Systems Costs
This benefit is due to avoiding unnecessary duplicative content in the Design phase's steps.

Benefit 7: Reduced Maintenance Systems Costs
This benefit is due to avoiding unnecessary duplicative content in the Design phase's steps.

Benefits Summary
The benefits of **reduced costs** in 3 through 7, in the earlier graphic and the text above, are all linked back to the successful accomplishment of the second benefit: the Increased Modular Design Reuse.

There is a logic behind all of this – a data logic. The PACT Data Logic is quite complex. Here next is the graphic for that Data Logic.

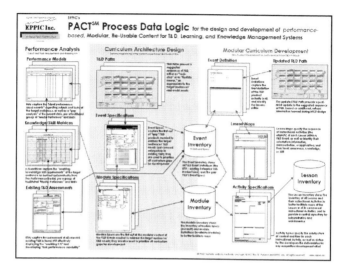

Go to www.eppic.biz and search for this
in a larger size when you get a chance.

The Data Logic is more related to Curriculum Architecture
Design efforts – and is not covered further in this book.

Case Examples & Testimonials

Here are four quick examples of what my Clients and I or
my team have achieved with the implementation of the
PACT Processes for their needs; plus one testimonial.

Case Example #1- Building Controls Industry

Project – Time to Performance

Client Situation - my Client is a marketplace leader in building controls solutions. Due to high growth, they needed to speed the "Time to Performance" for critical field positions, and certify jobholders for certain critical job performance capabilities. The project was to produce a qualification system, including integrated development and qualification Paths for nine field audiences, to impact "Time to Performance" plus develop Performance Tests.

Response – was to conduct analysis and design activities and developed classroom and on-the-job support tools, a battery of certification/qualification tests that were all Performance Tests (no written tests), and the administrative systems to support rollout and ongoing management of the system in the field and at headquarters.

Client Results - field acceptance and use of the program, along with results reported by the users, led to an internal President's Quality Award.

The "Time to Performance" program has been demanded by Siemens' Asian operations, and won an internal award.

Case Example 2 – Telecommunications Industry

Project – Product Management Process Training – Basic Skills

Client Situation - in 1986, AT&T Network Systems (now Lucent-Alcatel) leadership determined that their 800 product planners/managers were in need of development due to the competitive pressures management foresaw coming as a result of deregulation and the then recent split-up of the Bell System.

Each product manager managed a diverse portfolio of more than 500,000 products. They were organized into five separate business units with unique and common characteristics and needs.

The job itself was configured differently within each sub-business unit depending on the
product's life-cycle position and the age of the technologies being used.

Each business unit had varied policies and procedures/practices.

These product planners themselves had very diverse educational and work experiences in their backgrounds. Some had little or no business or financial knowledge.

Response - I was asked to conduct the analysis and design of an entire curriculum to address the varied needs of the target audiences, both existing employees and new hires.

Our Performance Model segmented the product planner job into eight components, each further subdivided in terms of how jobs were then currently configured. That Curriculum

Architecture Design (CAD) effort reused more than 60 existing courses from within the AT&T system, and specified just under 60 gap T&D Events.

Working with a Project Steering Team composed of top managers from each of the business units, we conducted further analysis and design and then developed their priority gaps from the 60 gaps. One gap from the 60 gaps in the overall CAD effort was the curriculum's keystone course: Product Management Process Training Basics.

I designed (post-CAD) that keystone course. It was an intensive, eight-day experience that taught business/ marketing/product planning, various financial analyses, meeting planning, cross-functional team management, and key legal/regulatory issues through a series of linked simulation exercises.

Client Results - the eight-day course was delivered by me and others 31 times between 1987 and 1994 (including five sessions in The Netherlands) before being reduced to a three-day version when taken over by the corporate training function.

The course won the 1989/90 ISPI (NSPI) Award of Excellence for "Finalist – Best Instructional Product" for generating a 457 percent return on the total investment as calculated by the client's financial organization, covering the initial development, the maintenance, and the delivery costs and returns in terms of speed to Performance Competence over the first two years.

Case Example 3 – Fleet Tire Management Industry

Project: Material Flow Workshop Development

Client Situation - my Client was the world leader in truck tire retreading, operating a global franchise network. They wanted to adopt the Synchronous Flow concept and techniques from the book *The Goal,* and teach them to their franchisees' owners and manufacturing operations managers in a workshop setting.

Response - I conducted analysis and design activities and developed a four-day classroom experience designed to teach the attendees the concepts, the tools and techniques, and how to implement "Material Flow" in their specific performance context.

Client Results - in one of the first shops trained, after only the first day back on the job, they were up and running at full speed using the new approach and produced 30 percent more product at a 20 percent cost savings. Results elsewhere have been similar.

Case Example 4 – Automotive Industry

Project - Material Fabrication Division Tool & Die Supervisors College Design

Client Situation - the Materials Fabrication Division of General Motors organization needed to further develop young technical school graduates to step quickly into the role of supervising older and more experienced UAW tool & die specialists. Contracts had already been signed with almost a dozen soon-to-be graduates to participate in the 18-month-long program envisioned and promised by MFD leadership. The delivery was to start within 6 months, and the project was just getting started.

Response - I facilitated a three-day analysis meeting, followed by a three-day Curriculum Architecture Design (CAD) design meeting to design the overall curricula, where 50 percent of the 18 months of chunked, performance-based content was to be spent on the floor observing and applying the content recently learned. The remainder was nine months of 40 hour/week group-paced instruction – conducted every-other week for the 18 month cycle.

I then facilitated (and modeled to recently trained PACT practitioners) my Modular Curriculum Development (MCD) design approach. The newly trained PACT practitioners then carried forward with the project, as many ISD teams ran in parallel to develop the materials one step ahead of delivery to the learners over the next 18 months.

Client Results - the final effort won the 1998 GM Chairman's Award as "one of the best of the best" global business initiatives, one of the few training efforts to win this accolade. MFD leadership was very pleased with the program's results and continues to use this program today.

There is a 12 minute video on my web site (www.eppic.biz) that my GM client created as a testimony to this award winning effort and about my ISD methods. Search for: "MC/MI Processes internally at General Motors University" to find that 12 minute video.

The testimonial that follows is from another GM contractor about this effort that won the GM Chairman's Award.

Testimonial

From a LinkedIn Recommendation:

"Guy Wallace was involved with my team in a project with GM to build a curriculum for stamping plant supervisors using his (MCD) processes. Guy's energy, experience, and skill, combined with the process made it possible for us to build an 18 month program that eventually won an award for our GM Client. Our Client really felt that a quality product was produced and that Guy and the team were excellent."

March 16, 2009

DeeAnn Caudel, *Director, General Physics*

Note: There are over 35 Recommendations for Guy W. Wallace on his LinkedIn profile.

Chapter Summary & Transition

This chapter was intended to provide you with the key benefits for the Enterprise for conducting MCD - Modular Curriculum Development projects for their most critical Target Audiences and on the ROI achieved through the 7 key benefits.

This chapter flows logically into the next, however your needs may cause you to want to skip around.

The following are the chapter titles and page numbers to assist you with your personal navigation needs.

Suggested Chapter Reflection & Reaction

I would suggest that prior to jumping into whichever chapter meets your needs that you give pause for a moment to reflect on the following and make some notes:

- Does this have applicability for me?

- What can I adopt from what I have read here?

- What are my potential needs for adaptation?

- What other issues do I see that I will need to address before embracing?

Please make note of your thoughts before proceeding.

Guy W. Wallace

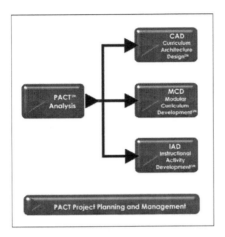

3 levels of ISD Methodologies
with common Analysis and
Project Planning & Management Methodologies.

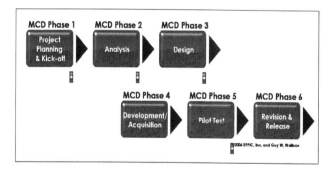

5 – THE MCD PROCESS PHASES, OUTPUTS AND TEAMS

Chapter Overview

This chapter is intended to provide you with an overview of the Phases for an MCD effort, a quick refresher review of the outputs per phases that have already been covered in earlier chapters – and an overview of the teams involved.

All of this in preparation for the deeper reviews in the succeeding chapters for each phase.

MCD POTS

The following graphic highlights the POTs: the Phases, Outputs and Teams of an MCD effort.

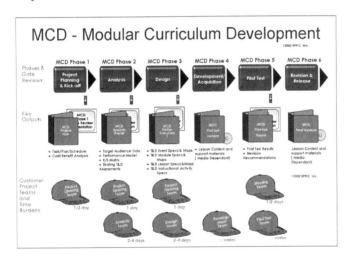

The 6 Phases are overviewed next.

Note that the phases can be combined if needed – and I have done so under the right circumstances.

Phase 1: Project Planning & Kick-off

In the first phase, the Customer (the requester of the project) and key Stakeholders are interviewed.

The Project Manager creates a Project Plan and presents it to the Project Steering Team for approval, deferral, modification, or rejection.

The Project Steering Team's decision to continue – and how – happen in the first gate in the Modular Curriculum Development processes and practices for Gate Review Meetings.

These efforts will be covered more extensively in chapter 6.

Phase 2: Analysis

In the second phase, the Analysis Team conducts four types of analysis to generate these four sets of analysis data:

- Target Audience data
- Performance Model data
- Enabling K/S data
- Existing T&D (L&D) Assessments data

The results are shared with the Project Steering Team in a second Gate Review Meeting. The Project Steering Team approves, modifies, or rejects the results of the analysis.

These efforts will be covered more extensively in chapter 7.

Phase 3: Design

During the third phase, the Design Team formulates a design for the Event or Events, per the project's scope.

Event Specs and Maps, Lesson Specs and Maps, and Instructional Activity Specs (no Maps) are produced as the Design Team is facilitated to process the analysis data.

This design data is presented to the Project Steering Team in the third Project Steering Team's Gate Review Meeting.

These efforts will be covered more extensively in chapter 8.

Phase 4: Development

During the fourth phase, the Development Team produces materials for the next phase's Pilot-Test. These materials might include:

- T&D materials (instructional, evaluation) and, depending on the deployment method
  - o Facilitator Guide and materials
  - o Participant Guide and materials
  - o Administrator Guide and materials
- Pilot-Test brochures and other marketing materials

These efforts will be covered more extensively in chapter 9.

Phase 5: Pilot-Test

During the fifth phase, the Pilot-Test Teams participate in the Instruction as close to "high-fidelity" as possible/feasible.

That means that if it is a classroom, instructor-led course, it is pilot-tested in that manner. If it is a self-paced e-learning course, it is pilot-tested in that manner. Sometimes the first delivery of the content is a stealth Pilot-Test. That happens when Clients dislike the idea of Pilot-Tests and Pilot-Testing.

Pilot-Test participants, including Learners and Facilitators (media/mode dependent) are debriefed post-Pilot and participate in other summative evaluations.

That evaluation data is then reviewed/scrutinized and used to create the Revision Results and Revision Recommendations, which are recommended to the Project Steering Team – for their approval or revisions – for the creation of the Revision Specifications – that will feed the last phase of an MCD effort.

These efforts will be covered more extensively in chapter 10.

Phase 6: Revision & Release

During the sixth phase, the Development Team takes the approved Revision Specifications and makes any and all updates to the Pilot-Test version of the materials.

The Instruction/Information is either Pilot-Tested again, or the materials are released to the on-going systems that are in place for ongoing deployment and/or access.

These efforts will be covered more extensively in chapter 11.

MCD Teams

The PACT Processes' structure spells out the teams and roles necessary to ensure the right people handle everything at the right time in the process.

In general, the same types of teams are used within Curriculum Architecture Design, Modular Curriculum Development, and Instructional Activity Development.

The major teams formed during a PACT Process project include

- Project Steering Team
- Analysis Team
- Design Team
- Development Team
- Pilot-Test Teams
- ISD Team

In addition, two other teams may be used.

- Analysis Review Teams
- Design Review Teams

Of course, there are a variety of roles on each of these teams. Those roles are covered in the discussions of the individual teams.

These will be covered more extensively in chapters 13 and 14.

Chapter Summary & Transition

This chapter was intended to provide you with an overview of the Phases for an MCD effort, a review of the outputs per phases – outputs that have already been covered in earlier chapters – and an overview of the teams involved.

All of this was presented in preparation for the deeper reviews of each of these phases, teams and outputs in the succeeding chapters of this book.

This chapter flows logically into the next, however your needs may cause you to want to skip around.

The following are the chapter titles and page numbers to assist you with your personal navigation needs.

Suggested Chapter Reflection & Reaction

I would suggest that prior to jumping into whichever chapter meets your needs that you give pause for a moment to reflect on the following and make some notes:

- Does this have applicability for me?

- What can I adopt from what I have read here?

- What are my potential needs for adaptation?

- What other issues do I see that I will need to address before embracing?

Please make note of your thoughts before proceeding.

Guy W. Wallace

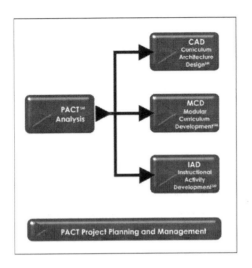

3 levels of ISD Methodologies
with common Analysis and
Project Planning & Management Methodologies.

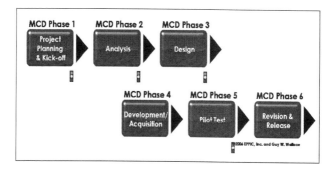

6 – PHASE 1: PROJECT PLANNING & KICK-OFF

Chapter Overview

This chapter is intended to provide you with details for the first of six phases of a MCD effort.

Note that the phases can be combined if needed. And that is a decision that happens in this first phase!

This first phase of MCD is where your agreement – formally as a contract – or less formally as an agreed upon plan of action – is created with your ISD Customers.

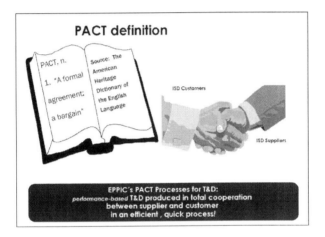

MCD Phase 1: Project Planning & Kick-Off

Phase 1 in Modular Curriculum Development, Project Planning & Kick-off, is where interviews are conducted, a Project Plan is drafted, and a Project Steering Team is assembled of Customers and key Stakeholders is assembled to

- Review and sanction the project.
- Modify the Project Plan or put the project on "temporary hold" and defer it.
- Cancel the project if it doesn't meet a priority business need.
- Handpick Analysis Team members.

In this phase, it is the Project Steering Team that handpicks or approves the members of the Analysis Team – not whomever the ISD Supplier can dig up.

Warning

It is at this point in the Modular Curriculum Development project that some L&D requesters want to forgo the Project Steering Team.

They want to make all the decisions themselves, to be in control or to save time. They don't want to be encumbered with a team to satisfy and bring to consensus.

From my viewpoint, the assembly of the right group of Stakeholders on the Project Steering Team is the singular critical factor for ultimate project success.

If Stakeholders are involved from day one, they'll typically be with you in the resourcing decisions to be made later.

They will affect whom you can get to work on your Analysis and Design Teams and free up the other critical resources, people, and nonhuman resources that your project will require.

On the other hand, if your ideal Project Steering Team members don't see the value in their participation on your project, chances are your project isn't very worthy at this time. And it may never be. And that's a good acid test itself.

How Formal Should You Be With Project Plans?

My bias is always toward the formality of creating, updating and providing a new Project Plan to the Project Steering

Team chairperson after each Phase.

I like to at least get a verbal go-ahead for the next phase. I never ask a Client to physically sign a piece of paper.

If there are schedule issues and cost issues, make sure the chairperson is aware of them all.

Manage the politics! Make sure you give your Customers all the information. Make sure you give them an opportunity to give you input and feedback *outside* the Project Steering Team meeting as well – meaning before the meeting.

One of the many Number 1 Rules I have learned over the decades is: allow no surprises!

Overview of MCD Phase 1: Project Planning & Kick-Off

Description – In this phase, project priorities, direction, and resources are defined. Potential issues and Stakeholder requirements are uncovered and planned for to ensure the success of remaining phases.

Key Activities/Tasks – A Project Steering Team meeting is held to review, critique, and revise plans for the proposed project. Commitments are obtained for personnel and resources.

Key Outputs – The outputs of this phase are a Project Plan and a Phase 1 kick-off presentation.

Tasks for MCD Phase 1: Project Planning & Kick-off

The tasks of Phase 1 for Modular Curriculum Development are organized into four sub-phases.

The structure of the four sub-phases is similar to most PACT Process phases: plan it, do it, review it, and revise it.

MCD Subphase 1.1 – Preproject Planning

In this sub-phase, the Customer and other key Stakeholders provide background data on needs, wants and desires, biases, etc. Based on this information, a Project Plan and Proposal are created.

One important question that must be answered in this sub-phase is whether the person or group who requested the T&D is its logical owner. The true logical owner must be identified.

MCD Subphase 1.2 – Initial Project Planning

In this sub-phase, the chairperson and members are recruited for the Project Steering Team. The Project Manager produces the first draft of a detailed Project Plan and Proposal. The Customer and the Project Steering Team review and sanction the plan, changing it as necessary.

The key is to have a "salable" Project Plan, one that will lead to a win-win success. The Project Manager's planning and sales skills need to be sharp!

MCD Subphase 1.3 – Phase 1 Gate Review

This sub-phase consists of preparing for and conducting a formal review of the Project Plan with the Project Steering Team. This review may take place at either a high or low level of detail, depending on the business needs and interests of team members and their tolerances for detail.

The purpose of the Gate Review Meeting is to identify team members who will serve throughout the project, identify resources needed to conduct subsequent phases, identify issues, and do additional planning.

It is also important to clarify the project's business drivers, rationale, intent, approach, schedule, and "burden" during this sub-phase.

Because the tasks in this sub-phase kick off the project with its key constituencies, the gate review is a chance for the Project Manager to set the tone for the remainder of the project by using good business skills.

MCD Subphase 1.4 – Phase 1 Completion and Transition

In this sub-phase, the Project Manager finalizes the Project Plan and Proposal. It is within the Proposal that resource dollar requirements are articulated and separated from the more widely distributed Project Plan. At this point, the Customer and ISD management sign off on the Project Plan and Proposal.

The Project Manager must ensure that the Project Steering Team chairperson fully understands and supports the specific project goals and deliverables, the collaborative approach, the task plan, and the time and schedule burdens on the rest of the organization in order to complete the project. There must be no surprises later on!

More Task Detail for MCD Phase 1: Project Planning & Kick-Off

Scan these detailed Task Listings for now – organized by the four sub-phases of Phase 1: Project Planning & Kick-Off, to simply become somewhat familiar with what's got to be done in this part of an MCD effort.

You will probably need to adapt this detailed listing – rather than adopt it for your context – when you are planning your first real project.

MCD Subphase 1.1 – Preproject Planning

1. ISD reviews the request for T&D coming from any request screening process used within the company. If the request is potentially appropriate for a Curriculum Architecture Design project, ISD management assigns a CAD Project Manager and plans for a CAD project. If the project is most appropriate for Modular Curriculum Development, ISD management assigns an MCD Project Manager and initiates the MCD project.

2. The request for the prospective Modular Curriculum Development project is reviewed with the original requester and other key Stakeholders using the PACT Process Client/Stakeholder Interview Guide to clarify
   - The Customer's business process and human performance situational needs
     - Problems and opportunities
     - Desired outcomes (training and other)

- The type of deployment platform desired for delivery
- Constraints of time, budget, and approach
- Non-training issues to be addressed
- Intended target audiences
- Existing T&D to be assessed for use
- Other key Stakeholders to be involved in the project along with their interest and level of involvement

3. The Project Manager clarifies with ISD management the logical owner of the project (if different from the original requester), and discusses the appropriateness of that individual for the role of Project Steering Team chairperson. With ISD organizational guidance, the Project Manager identifies all other appropriate organizational interfaces and all key Stakeholders for potential project involvement as members of the Project Steering Team or other MCD project teams.

4. The Project Manager clarifies with the original requester any issues regarding the project's logical ownership, if the owner is different from the requester. The Project Manager ensures the requester's continued involvement (if desired) on the Project Steering Team.

5. The Project Manager contacts the logical owner regarding the project to determine whether the owner wishes to be involved. The Project Manager recruits the logical owner as the Project Steering Team chairperson, if appropriate. If not, the Project Manager contacts the next logical candidate.

6. The Project Manager conducts any additional preliminary interviews as needed to complete an initial draft Project Plan/Proposal.

MCD Subphase 1.2 – Initial Project Planning

1. Using the Project Plan/Proposal templates, the Project Manager creates a draft Project Plan and Proposal and forwards it to ISD leadership for review. (The templates are available through the PACT Processes Technology Transfer.)

2. ISD leadership conducts a detailed review of the draft Project Plan/Proposal and identifies any issues for resolution.

3. ISD leadership provides feedback via a formal presentation or verbal discussion regarding the draft Project Plan. ISD leadership also identifies key Stakeholders for potential inclusion on the Project Steering Team.

4. The Project Manager updates the Project Plan/Proposal based on feedback from ISD leadership, and presents the plan to the Customer (the original requester or logical owner) for preliminary review.

5. The Customer conducts a detailed review of the draft Project Plan/Proposal and identifies any issues for resolution. The Customer also identifies key Stakeholders for interviewing and potential inclusion on the Project Steering Team.

6. During a preliminary but formal presentation, or during verbal discussion, the Customer provides feedback regarding the draft Project Plan/Proposal.

7. The Project Manager updates the Project Plan/Proposal based on the feedback from the Customer.

8. The Customer selects additional Project Steering Team members (as appropriate) and recruits and orients each member to the major project issues and goals, explaining as well the responsibilities of Project

Steering Team members. The Customer is assisted in this task by ISD leadership or the MCD Project Manager assigned.

MCD Subphase 1.3 – Phase 1 Gate Review

1. The Project Manager coordinates all logistics for the Phase 1 Project Steering Team Gate Review Meeting, including
   - Meeting method and location, along with dates and times
   - Arrangements for meeting materials, equipment, and food and beverage
   - Invitations and communications about
     - Date, time, location, and directions
     - Accommodations for travel, living, meals, etc.
     - The project, meeting purpose, outputs, process, specific roles, and any preparations required on the part of meeting participants
2. The Project Manager confirms the attendance of all key participants and the completion of all assigned prework immediately prior to the Project Steering Team Gate Review Meeting.
3. The Project Manager prepares all meeting materials and briefs additional meeting participants (as needed) for the Project Steering Team Phase 1 gate review. Preparations include
   - Agendas
   - Gate review presentation materials and handout materials
   - Assignments
   - Briefings
4. The Project Manager conducts a two- to four-hour Project Steering Team Phase 1 Gate Review Meeting to

- Review the project purpose, business drivers, approach, process, deliverables, and schedule for key milestones.
- Review the Project Plan details and modify as needed.
- Identify all members of the Analysis Team.
- Identify the time burdens and schedule requirements for all project personnel.
- Identify all source materials, references, and resources for data on
  - Target audiences
  - Business processes
  - Human performance requirements
  - Existing T&D
- Identify all other key issues (problems, opportunities, goals, constraints, etc.).
- Discuss the preliminary
  - Deployment Strategy and Plan
  - Development /Acquisition Planning Strategy and Plan
  - Evaluation Strategy and Plan
- Identify the non-training informational outputs from the Analysis Phase that will be presented and reviewed in the Phase 2 analysis outputs and gate review by the Project Steering Team.
- Set the schedule for all remaining Project Steering Team Gate Review Meetings, as appropriate.
- Assess the phase completion status using the Phase 1 exit criteria.

MCD Subphase 1.4 – Phase 1 Completion and Transition

1. The Project Manager updates the Modular Curriculum Development Project Plan/Proposal and forwards the updated version to all Project Steering Team members and all ISD management (as appropriate). Also on the distribution list: other assigned or relevant individuals with a need to know.

2. The Project Manager obtains sign-offs from the Customer (the Project Steering Team chairperson) and ISD management (as appropriate).

3. The Project Manager gathers all project resource materials and holds them in readiness for the Analyst assigned to the project.

The Project Plan & Proposal

The following graphic presents my outline for a Project Plan. A Detailed Project Plan.

If your Clients dislikes detailed Project Plans – then create the detailed version for yourself – and then dumb it down for those with less tolerance for planning at the detailed level.

Note: I always separate the Project Plan from the Proposal – where the price information goes – so that there is no hesitation on sharing the Project Plan with everyone concerned with the project.

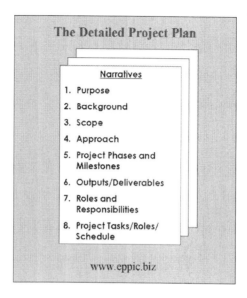

Task Charts

I don't use sophisticated Project Planning software when planning my PACT Projects. I use a template of the Tasks presented earlier in this chapter – and in the next 3 chapters on the three phases that follow Project Planning & Kick-Off – and put my estimates of the touch time required – plus or minus 25% - as they are educated guesses, informed guesses.

Plus I put in the dates, but only for the key meetings.

I do not schedule each and every task in the plan.

Here is an example of that format.

Example Task Chart
The Detailed Project Plan

Project Tasks	Estimated Days Required							Schedule	
	EPPIC, Inc.			TMC Corporation					
	GW	CS	PS	PM	PT	PP	Other (each)	Start	End
1. Identify, contact, and recruit three to five "Project Team" members for the Working Committee to provide input, critique, and support to the Analysis, Design, Development, and Pilot Testing effort	--	--	--	2.0	--	--	--		
2. Coordinate logistics for Task 4 •Room arrangements •Equipment arrangements •Invitations and information to attendees •Meals/refreshments •Final confirmation of invited attendees' intentions to attend	0.25	--	--	1.0	--	--	--		
3. Prepare to conduct Task 4 •Meeting process design •Presentation preparation •"Straw" models/starter prototypes for use in Task 4	1.0	2.0	2.0	--	--	--	--		

KEY: EPPIC, Inc.   TMC Corporation
          GW = Guy Wallace   PM = Project manager
          CS = Consultant Support   PT = Project Team
          PS = Production Support PP = Pilot Participants									

www.eppic.biz

But where does the information for the Project Plan comes from?

It comes from the inputs and feedback from the Clients – the Customer and the Stakeholders.

The following is my Interview Guide for those initial pre-planning efforts.

This would be used by the ISD Supplier person serving in the Role of the PACT Project Manager/ Planner.

Stakeholder Interview & Review Guide – Part 1

Project Plan Development Guide

Problem/Opportunity Background
Customer

- Who is/are the Customer(s)?
  - Names, titles, organizations

- Who is/are the (potential) sponsor(s)?
  - Names, titles, organizations

- Who are the other key Stakeholders?
  - Names, titles, organizations

Problem/Opportunity Statement

- What is the specific problem/opportunity?
  - Who, what, where, when, why regarding the symptoms?
  - What are the key metrics (measures) required by each, and what is the actual versus desired performance?
  - Is the cause known or suspected?
  - How will solving the problem benefit the company, organization, Stakeholders, etc.?

- Is the solution being prescribed by the Customer?
  - How flexible and receptive are they to other solutions or redefining the problem?

  - What is the background related to this project?
    - What has led up to this?

- What are the stimuli (stimulus) for undertaking the project?
- Why is this being addressed now?
- What other issues and initiatives will impact this project?
- What other issues and initiatives will be impacted by this project?

Project Overview

T&D Project Objectives
- What specifically should the project accomplish?
  - What is to be produced and for whom?
  - How will it be measured, in general?

Project Success Criteria
- What are all the success criteria or metrics per key Stakeholder group?
- Over what period of time should we expect to gain improvement?

Evaluation Plan
- What is the plan for conducting an evaluation of the training and development and the results of the project?
  - Who will conduct the effort?
  - What will be produced and to whom will it be distributed?

Deployment Plan
- How will the training and development be deployed?
- By whom?
- How often?

Development Plan

- Who are the Subject Matter Experts or Master Performers?
- Are/will they be available to support the development effort?
- What are the constraints on their time and availability?
- Do materials and information currently exist?

Project Scope/Deliverables/Approach/Roles
Scope

- What defines the beginning and end points for this project?
  - Project activities
  - Calendar/schedule
- What is included within the scope of the project?
  - Target populations
  - Process(es) or performance boundaries
  - Types of consulting services
- What should be explicitly excluded from the scope of the project?

Deliverables

- What specifically is to be produced and delivered as a part of the project?
  - Reports, presentations, etc.
- How many iterations are expected for each deliverable?
  - Initial draft
  - Number of additional drafts/updates
- What software packages (and version) will be used to produce the outputs?
- What format, structure, and packaging rules will be followed (as appropriate) for each of the deliverables?

Approach

- Who will own the ongoing maintenance of the deliverables?
- What key methods will be employed to conduct the various activities of the project?
    - Literature research
    - Surveys (phone or written)
    - Interviews (with whom)
    - Group meetings (with whom and for what purposes)
    - Etc.

Roles and Responsibilities

- What are the key roles (role sets) involved in the project?
    - Sponsor
    - Customer Project Manager
    - Steering Teams
    - Analysis Teams
    - Design Teams
    - Pilot-Test Teams
    - Etc.
- What are the specific responsibilities for each of the roles?
    - To direct
    - To approve/reject
    - To review
    - To provide input

ISD Supplier Staff Backgrounds

- What are the following for each staff member to be assigned to the project?
    - Name, title, organization
    - Assigned project role
    - Credentials (education, work experience, publications, etc.)

Project Tasks/Assignments/Schedule
Task Charts

- What is the reaction to the standard phases for conducting this type of project?
- What should be the dates for key project milestones that are acceptable?
- What are the key outputs per phase?
- What are the key tasks/activities per phase?
- Which role is needed to be involved in which project tasks?
- What are the key schedule dates for key project tasks (review meetings, etc.)?

Get the answers to the above questions from the ISD Customers and Stakeholders for the content needed for your documented Project Plan.

Next: the Proposal development questions to be answered by the ISD Suppliers.

Stakeholder Interview & Review Guide – Part 2

Proposal Development Guide

Project Cost Summary
- Total project cost
  - Estimated or fixed fee?

Cost Breakdown

ISD Supplier Staff Costs
- Number of days of involvement required by CADI staff
- Rate per day

Outside Contractor Costs
- Number of days of involvement required by outside contractor

Travel and Living
- Expenses
- How many trips will be required?
- Average airfare expected
- Number of days out of town
- Cost per day for food, lodging, ground travel, and miscellaneous expenses

Materials
- What materials will be consumed in the course of the project?
  - Report binders, tabs, and paper
  - Presentation materials
  - Etc.

Extraordinary Support Services

- What additional services will be consumed in the course of the project that are not covered by the daily rates of the staff member?
- Word processing temporaries
- Graphic services
- Shipping
- Printing
- Other duplication
- Etc.

Note that this set of questions, to be answered by the Project Planner – after they interviewed and/or confirmed what they think they already know – parallels my previously presented outline for both the Project Plan and the Proposal.

And remember the words of Ike!

It is the act of planning and not the actual plan that is the critical thing.

However, I prefer to plan at a detailed level for all ISD efforts – and believe and have proven in hundreds of projects – that with the appropriate collaboration with my

Clients - that the plans for MCD efforts do not have to change at all.

The only changes I've ever experienced in over 30 years of planning MCD-type efforts is when the schedule had to be slipped – and that was always due to the Client asking me to do so for their convenience. Not because we on the ISD Supplier side where running behind.

Other MCD Phase Configurations

The following are typical adaptations for the phases of MCD efforts.

This configuration might be used when the MCD effort follows a CAD – Curriculum Architecture design effort and the analysis and design from that effort is deemed detailed enough to short-cut those phases and combine them.

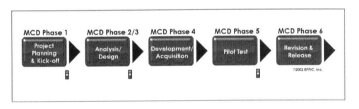

Note that I do not "lose" the Phase numbers in this reconfiguration.

This next configuration might be used when Pilot-Testing is deemed unnecessary – perhaps after the type of content has been developed previously (say for lots of product knowledge content) and the process is thought to then be reliable enough – and that any errors would be caught using other means (than a formal Pilot-Test).

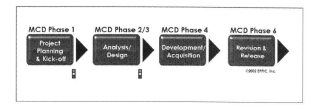

Note again that "Phase 5" is missing – but that Phase 6 is still Phase 6.

Chapter Summary & Transition

This chapter was intended to present the details of Phase 1: Project Planning & Kick-Off for an MCD effort.

This chapter flows logically into the next, Phase 2, however your needs may cause you to want to skip around.

The following are the chapter titles and page numbers to assist you with your personal navigation needs.

Suggested Chapter Reflection & Reaction

I would suggest that prior to jumping into whichever chapter meets your needs that you give pause for a moment to reflect on the following and make some notes:

- Does this have applicability for me?

- What can I adopt from what I have read here?

- What are my potential needs for adaptation?

- What other issues do I see that I will need to address before embracing?

Please make note of your thoughts before proceeding.

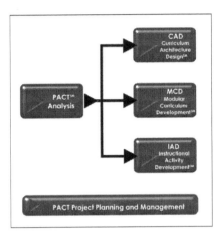

3 levels of ISD Methodologies
with common Analysis and
Project Planning & Management Methodologies.

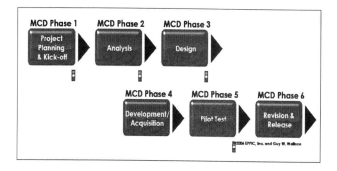

7 – PHASE 2: ANALYSIS

Chapter Overview

This chapter is intended to provide you details about Phase 2 of an MCD effort.

Warning: There is a lot of detail here to be covered.

Again, the phases can be combined if that is what is needed in your context.

MCD Phase 2: Analysis

During Phase 2: Analysis, target audience data is gathered and preparations and logistics are conducted for the Analysis Team meeting.

If the Modular Curriculum Development project follows a Curriculum Architecture Design project, the CAD data is validated and an Analysis Team meeting is conducted to generate more detail for the Performance Model and Knowledge/Skill Matrices. If not, then that begins with a blank set of pages.

After the Analysis Team meeting, all relevant existing training is assessed to see if it fits the training needs documented in the Performance Model and Knowledge/ Skill Matrices.

This data is then documented in an Analysis Report, which is presented during the Project Steering Team Gate Review Meeting for Phase 2.

The analysis data must be approved in that meeting before the Design Phase begins.

Overview of Phase 2: Analysis

Description – This phase establishes a common view of personnel, performance requirements, knowledge and skill requirements, and appropriateness and completeness of any existing training.

This view will form the basis for the training design.

Key Activities/Tasks – Target audience demographics are gathered, and the PACT Analyst conducts a two-to-four-day analysis meeting with Master Performers from the target population.

During this meeting the Analysis Team identifies job requirements, performance gaps, and knowledge and skill requirements.

Existing T&D is then assessed for fit and its reuse potential.

Finally, the Project Steering Team reviews the analysis data in a Gate Review Meeting.

Key Outputs – Outputs of this phase include the following:

- Phase 2 Analysis Team Kick-Off presentation
- Phase 2 Project Steering Team Gate Review Meeting presentation
- Phase 2 Analysis Report
  - Target Audience Data
  - Performance Model
  - Knowledge/Skill Matrix
  - Existing T&D Assessments

Tasks for MCD Phase 2 – Analysis

The tasks of Phase 2 for Modular Curriculum
Development are organized into four sub-phases.

MCD Subphase 2.1 – Pre-analysis Planning, Data Gathering, and Preparation

The goal of this sub-phase is to ensure that key players in the next sub-phases are fully prepared to conduct the activities of the project.

In particular, the Analyst reviews materials and conducts individual interviews as required.

MCD Subphase 2.2 – Analysis Process and Documentation

In this sub-phase, the Analyst and the Analysis Team conduct the Analysis Team meeting and embellish the analysis data after the meeting.

All existing T&D is assessed for its fit to the project's stated needs.

Finally, activities in this sub-phase are documented in the Analysis Report and presented during the Project Steering Team Gate Review Meeting.

MCD Subphase 2.3 – Phase 2 Gate Review

The major activity in this sub-phase is a review of the analysis data with the Project Steering Team.

The analysis data may be voluminous; the time available for the Project Steering Team meeting may be short.

Therefore, the goal of the Project Manager and Analyst is to ensure the quality, completeness, and accuracy of the data in an expedient manner.

At this point, ISD practitioners involved in the project should have a certain comfort level with the analysis data, and they might even know where there are holes in the data or where the Analysis Team was not in consensus.

It's up to the ISD practitioners to focus the Project Steering Team on these problem areas and get them resolved.

The goal is to either get the issues resolved, or to walk away with a strategy and specific plans to get them resolved in time for their use during the next phase.

After that it's too late, and rework is probably guaranteed.

MCD Subphase 2.4 – Phase 2 Completion and Transition

The goal of this sub-phase is to wrap up the phase and ensure that the Project Steering Team chairperson is still "on board."

This is especially necessary if the Project Plan needs to be changed due to new information or new, unanticipated circumstances. Updates are made to the Analysis Report and data based on the feedback from the Project Steering Team.

More Task Detail for Phase 2: Analysis

Scan these detailed Task Listings for now – organized by the four sub-phases of Phase 2: Analysis, to simply become somewhat familiar with what's got to be done in this part of an MCD effort.

You will probably need to adapt this detailed listing – rather than adopt it for your context – when you are planning your first real project.

MCD Subphase 2.1 – Pre-analysis Planning, Data Gathering, and Preparation

1. The Project Manager reviews the project with the newly assigned Analyst (as appropriate) and provides all resource materials for the Analyst's orientation.
2. The Analyst reviews the resource materials provided, obtaining additional materials and clarifying as necessary by phone or in person.
3. The Analyst coordinates logistics for all individual interviews, as needed. The Analyst

   • Contacts all interview participants and orients them to the project's purpose, outputs, process, and their specific roles
   • Establishes meeting methods, locations, dates, and times
4. The Analyst prepares for and then conducts individual interviews.
5. The Analyst prepares, as appropriate, any analysis straw models for use in the analysis process, using blank templates for creating initial drafts of

   • The Performance Model
   • The Knowledge/Skill Matrices

MCD Subphase 2.2 – Analysis Process and Documentation

1. The Analyst gathers data and documents the data on the Target Audience Data template or its equivalent.

The data comes from sources identified by the Project Steering Team in the Phase 1 Gate Review Meeting, or from Human Resources, Personnel, or the ISD organizations.

2. The Project Manager coordinates all logistics for the Phase 2 Analysis Team meeting, including

   • Meeting method, location, dates, and times

   • Arrangements for meeting materials, equipment, and food and beverage

   • Invitations and communications about
     - Date, time, location, and directions
     - Accommodations for travel, living, meals, etc.
     - The project, meeting purpose, outputs, process, specific roles, and any preparations required on the part of meeting participants

3. The Project Manager confirms attendance of all key participants and completion of all assigned prework immediately prior to the Analysis Team meeting.

4. The Project Manager and Analyst prepare all meeting materials and orient any additional project staff participants for the upcoming Analysis Team meeting. The following are prepared, as appropriate:

   • Agendas

   • Analysis Team presentation materials and all handout materials

   • Assignments

   • Briefings

5. The Analyst conducts the analysis process via either a multiday Analysis Team meeting or via meetings with individual Analysis Team members. The Analyst

   • Orients the team members to the project and the meeting

   • Creates (or edits or adds detail to) the Performance Model

- Derives the detailed enabling Knowledge and Skills, placing them on the Knowledge/Skill Matrices
- Assesses the work of the team and identifies any open issues for the Project Steering Team to address

6. The Analyst (with the help of team members and others familiar with the training) conducts assessments of any and all existing T&D programs and materials via searches in the T&D databases, examination of paper files, and discussions with key ISD personnel. The Analyst documents all findings using the Existing T&D Assessment templates.

7. The Analyst documents all analysis data, meeting results, and interview outputs. The Analyst develops the draft Analysis Report with the help of "go-by's" and templates. Components of the report include

- Target Audience Data
- Performance Model
- Knowledge/Skill Matrix
- Existing T&D Assessments

8. The Analyst produces the draft Analysis Report. The Project Manager or Analyst may forward copies of the report to ISD management and to the Project Steering Team for review prior to the Project Steering Team Gate Review Meeting.

MCD Subphase 2.3 – Phase 2 Gate Review

1. The Project Manager and Analyst prepare meeting materials and orient new participants for their role in the Project Steering Team Gate Review Meeting. The Project Manager and Analyst prepare, as appropriate, the following:

- Agendas
- Gate review presentation materials and all handout materials

- Assignments
- Briefings

2. The Project Manager coordinates all logistics for the Phase 2 Project Steering Team Gate Review Meeting, including

- Meeting method, location, dates, and times
- Arrangements for meeting materials, equipment, and food and beverage
- Invitations and communications about
  - Date, time, location, and directions
  - Accommodations for travel, living, meals, etc.
  - The project, meeting purpose, outputs, process, specific roles, and any preparations required on the part of meeting participants

3. The Project Manager confirms attendance of all key participants and the completion of all assigned prework immediately prior to the Project Steering Team meeting.

4. The Project Manager and Analyst conduct an eight-hour Project Steering Team Gate Review Meeting to

- Review the project purpose, business drivers, approach, process, deliverables, and schedule for key milestones.
- Review all actuals compared to plan, the rationale for all deviations, and the implications for the project's cost and schedule performance.
- Review the analysis data or summaries regarding
  - The Target Audience Data
  - Performance Models and requirements
  - Enabling Knowledge and Skills
  - Existing T&D Assessments
- Review non-training issues.
- Identify all other key project issues (problems, opportunities, goals, constraints, etc.).

- Discuss the preliminary
  - Deployment Strategy and Plan
  - Development/Acquisition Strategy and Plan
  - Evaluation Strategy and Plan
- Recommend and discuss the alternative delivery and deployment platforms appropriate for the content and audiences. Discuss the
  - Strategies, tactics, and key implications of each deployment platform
    - Deployment platform orientations and infrastructure requirements
    - Assessment of the current deployment infrastructure system's capability to handle the volume projections
    - Instructional effectiveness of the deployment platform for the type of learning (Knowledge/Skill) to be deployed
    - Initial development and deployment cost projections
- Select the deployment platform to be used in Phase 3: Design.
- Name two or three members for the Design Team from the membership of the Analysis Team, or confirm the recommendations from the ISD organization. Select a Design Team lead. Ensure qualifications of all Design Team members as
  - Subject Matter Experts (SMEs)
  - Master Performers (MPs)
- Assess the phase completion status using Phase 2 exit criteria.

MCD Subphase 2.4 – Phase 2 Completion and Transition

1. The Project Manager determines any changes required to the Analysis Report and the Project Plan/Proposal, and resolves any staffing issues for the next phase.
2. The Analyst updates the Analysis Report and Project Plan/Proposal (as needed) based on the Project Steering Team meeting and decisions. The plan and report are forwarded to all appropriate project participants and key Stakeholders.
3. The Project Manager obtains sign-offs from ISD management and from the Customer (the Project Steering Team chairperson).
4. The Project Manager gathers all project resource materials and holds them for the assigned Designer's use.

Analysis – But Without Paralysis

All too often, Training & Development content is designed without the benefits of good analysis data, driven instead to meet some arbitrary specifications that usually focus on *content topics* rather than *performance*.

Or worse, learning objectives are quickly generated off the tops of the heads of the key Clients as a way of heading off the dreaded *analysis paralysis*.

When this happens, the realities of the job performance requirements are not factored into the design. As a result, T&D suffers, learning suffers, and the chance to improve business process performance suffers. ROI goes negative, etc.

Too many organizations are unwilling to commit the time and resources necessary to perform a good set of analyses. The corporate thought process usually is: *Avoid analysis paralysis. Just do it.*

Unfortunately, this bias toward haste typically guarantees waste down the road.

What is needed is a lean approach to the analysis effort that Clients can see is quick, adds value to the process, and is subject to their managerial oversight and control.

To design successful, performance-based T&D, the ISD organization must have a solid understanding of

- The individuals who will be performing
- The specific performance required
- The level of performance currently being achieved
- The Knowledge and Skills that enable mastery-level performance
- The strengths and weaknesses of any current T&D and what might be salvaged from that T&D

This can only come through credible, thoughtful, and documented analysis. It does not need to be long, drawn-out, or complex. It should be *lean* and *quick*.

The PACT Analysis Process

The second phase of each of the three PACT Processes — Curriculum Architecture Design, Modular Curriculum Development, and Instructional Activity Development — is Analysis.

The PACT Analysis process addresses the issues and needs described above.

The four key analytic **methods** used in Phase 2 of each of the PACT Processes are

- Analyzing Target Audience Data
- Performance Modeling
- Knowledge/Skill Analysis
- Assessing Existing T&D

The goal of the PACT Project Manager and the Analyst is to collect the analysis information, understand it, communicate it to key Customers and key Stakeholders, and have the Project Steering Team "buy it" or revise it before proceeding to use it in design.

The heart of the PACT Processes for T&D, the drivers that keep T&D performance-based, are the Performance Models that lead to performance-based Knowledge/Skill Matrices.

Analysis of both the performance requirements and the enabling Knowledge/Skills is done quickly and effectively in the PACT methodology – in a Group Process effort.

The resulting data drives the design at the macro-level (Curriculum Architecture Design), midlevel (Modular Curriculum Development), and micro-level (Instructional Activity Development) of the PACT Processes.

Additional analyses in the second phase of each of the PACT Processes gather data and generate insights into the target audiences' demographics and an assessment of reuse potential for any existing content.

The Target Audience Data helps ISD professionals better understand their Customers at the Learner level.

Project members also assess all existing T&D for its functional fit to the newly defined, performance-based needs for T&D; this is the Existing T&D Assessment.

Why Gather Target Audience Data?

"Know thy Customer" applies to T&D as well as it does to any consumer product venture. For that reason, gathering Target Audience Data is one of the four types of PACT Analyses covered in this section of the book.

A good picture of the audience allows project team members to complete successfully the Analysis and Design Phases of Curriculum Architecture Design, Modular Curriculum Development, and Instructional Activity Development.

The reason for collecting data about the target audience is to understand the Customers for the T&D. This ensures that the eventual design (done in Phase 3 of each of the PACT Processes) is appropriate to the learners' background and the knowledge, skill, and experience they bring to the training.

Just as marketers need to understand the Customers for their products, the PACT Project Manager and Analyst must understand who their Customers are. Specifically, they're interested in the primary, secondary, and even tertiary target audiences.

Depending on the experience the Analyst and the ISD organization have with the target audience and the work environment, quite a bit may already be known about the target audience – and this part of the analysis may be skipped.

Again, "skipped" if it is already known by all involved in the effort to be undertaken. The more knowledge about the target audiences available at the start of a PACT Process, the less new data is needed. If the Analyst's understandings are based on past experiences, the Analyst may simply need to confirm and update those understandings.

Knowing what can safely be assumed and what cannot be assumed is critical. For example

- Does the audience generally have degrees in electrical engineering and experience working in the manufacturing factories, or is there a mixed bag of educational and work experience backgrounds?
- Do audience members exist as "one-sies" and "two-sies" across the organizational landscape—at the 87 sales offices in 14 countries—or are they all in one building at headquarters?
- Do all Target Audience members have Masters of Business Administration?
- Do they all speak and read "Business English" well enough?

The goal of gathering Target Audience Data is not to pin down audience characteristics 100 percent, but rather to get a feel for the audience. Know thy Customer!

Components of the Target Audience Data

Components of the Target Audience Data vary depending on the particular project. Data points might include:

- Audience job titles
- Audience size, historical trends, and future expectations regarding size
- Audience demographics—where jobholders are geographically
- Audience educational backgrounds
- Audience work/industry experiences

Turnover rates and other key data are also important in their potential impact to the Design Phase's activities and decisions.

T&D requesters may say that the population is not growing or will not grow over time, but the Analyst may discover that the stable size of the audience hides the fact that the Client has a significant turnover rate.

The implication for training is that the numbers of new learners will not necessarily diminish over the years, and there will be a continuous stream of folks to train (unless the Client fixes the cause of the high turnover).

The Analyst and Project Manager needs to understand the reality of turnover in order to formulate initial packaging and deployment strategies for the T&D. To reduce life-cycle costs.

The Analyst also needs to know the range of educational levels and work experiences of the targeted Customers of Content. Information on audience educational backgrounds is obviously crucial to designing and building flexible T&D that allows the Learners to pass over things they already know – of won't need to know for their specific job assignment. The amount of work experience audience members have in the industry also will affect design and development.

Future expectations regarding the audience size are nice to know. However, getting this data from business leaders may be difficult due to concerns over leaking proprietary business strategies. No responsible business leader will hand over sensitive and potentially damaging data that has a link to critical business strategy, even if withholding the data has a negative effect on T&D.

If the business leaders are going to close an operation, get out of a line of business, or build up capacity in a certain area, the Analyst may be out of luck in obtaining accurate data on future expectations concerning audience size.

This situation can be dealt with by getting organizational leaders to participate in the PACT Processes via the Project Steering Team – and allowing them to make certain decision without having to explain those decisions. Leaders sometimes need to be able to make decisions without sharing all of their rationale. These decision points occur in the MCD Design Phase of PACT.

The geographic locations of the audience is important for at least two reasons. First, it may affect how the T&D is deployed. And second, if an audience is widely dispersed, it may suggest assembling a geographically divergent Analysis Review Team to ensure input and buy-in from the various locations. Can the Analyst safely *assume* anything about the target audience? What the Analyst can safely assume about audience members and will hand off to the Designer will have a major impact on the content configuration created in the downstream activities later – in the MCD Design Phase!

Potential Source	Potential Data	Typical Issues
HR/Personnel Departments	• Current actual figures on population sizes, historical trends, education and experience backgrounds, and records of previous T&D experiences	• A Human Resources Information System may or may not exist and may or may not sort to the Analyst's needs • Access may be denied • Data may not be accurate

Potential Source	Potential Data	Typical Issues
T&D requester	• Same as above • Future plans impacting growth/shrinking of the workforce, shifts geographically, etc.	• Access may be denied due to marketplace issues and strategic plan sensitivity
Other key Stakeholders	• Same as above	• Access may be denied

The typical and logical sources may be Human Resources or the Personnel Department.

However, sometimes those sources don't have the data readily available, and extracting it from their systems can be problematic.

And sometimes the T&D requester or leadership of the business unit that will be affected by the T&D resists sharing data unless they understand that the Analyst's need to know, along with the costs associated with the Analyst's ignorance, are neither minor nor manageable.

Conducting the Target Audience Data Analysis

To conduct the Target Audience Data analysis, either the Analyst or Project Manager (assume it's the Analyst) has three main alternatives. The Analyst may use one of these or all three.

First, the Analyst can ask the Customer representatives if they have this data, are willing to share it, or where else the demographic insights can be found. The Analyst must be prepared to explain why, where, and when he or she needs this data. Another way to get much of the Target Audience Data is to find out whether Project Steering Team members—as Customer representatives—are likely to have it, then to ask them during the Phase 1 Gate Review Meeting.

Second, the Analyst can meet with an HR/personnel representative to explain project needs and ask for data.

A **third** way is to ask Analysis Team members during the Analysis Team meeting.

How much detail should the Analyst gather at this point? Knowing that there are 123 sales reps, and that during the next week two of them will be let go and then three hired, is far too much detail.

Knowing there are between 100 and 150 is close enough. But knowing that the sales reps are located in 25 sales offices versus two could make a large impact in the configuration, packaging, and deployment of the T&D.

And knowing that due to recent acquisitions, job titles vary greatly but job performance is basically consistent will help tremendously in other analysis and later design efforts.

The insights gained from the Target Audience Data effort are used to

- Clarify role responsibilities in the Performance Model effort of the Analysis Phase.
- Impact the design configuration of T&D content.
- Select appropriate deployment methods for Events and Modules later in the Design Phases of Curriculum Architecture Design or Modular

Curriculum Development.

Coming up in the next chapter is coverage of the Performance Model and its use during the PACT Analysis Process.

About Performance Models

The heart of the analysis portion of the PACT Processes is the Performance Model. It allows the T&D to be performance-based. Data built into the Performance Model permeates all remaining PACT Processes – as Performance Competence drives all measures of success – all learning objectives and evaluations.

While each type of analysis is important, the single key to PACT Process success is performance analysis as documented through the Performance Model.

Performance Modeling pins down the requirements of the performers within the scope of the intended project and creates Performance Models.

The Performance Model is the device used to capture ideal performance requirements, and it provides a way to identify gaps from ideal performance.

The Performance Model, generated with the Analysis Team, provides an illustration of both ideal performance – and actual performance via a gap analysis.

The information in the left half of a Performance Model describes *ideal* performance. This information includes

- Area of Performance (AoP, also called a *segment* of performance)

- Outputs produced and their measures
- Tasks performed
- Roles and responsibilities for task performance

Measures and standards of performance (at the level of Area of Performance, output, or task)

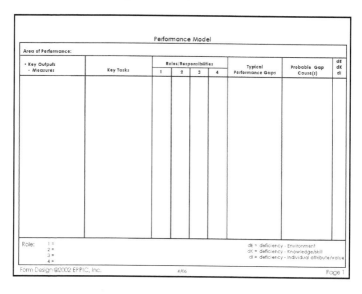

The information in the right half of a Performance Model also captures and articulates *real* performance via a gap analysis, including

- Typical performance gaps (where standards for measures at any level are *typically* not being met by job incumbents)
- Probable causes of those gaps
- Differentiation of those causes into one or more of three categories of deficiency
  - o dE: deficiency of environmental support
  - o dK: deficiency of Knowledge and Skills
  - o dI: deficiency of individual attributes and values

These deficiency types are explained in more detail later.

Performance Models may be developed for an entire organization, a function, a job, a major or minor task, or a business process.

Areas of Performance

Each Performance Model chart represents one Area of Performance. Areas of Performance are major chunks or macro-level responsibilities within a job; they segment performance within the scope of the project.

The trickiest part of building a Performance Model is defining a good set of Areas of Performance.

To define them well, the facilitator must know how Areas of Performance are used in the downstream PACT Process, and also how the information in the Areas of Performance fits in with the Knowledge/Skill analysis methodology and the design methodology.

A facilitator needs practice, intuition, and good judgment to carve out Areas of Performance from the performance jungle.

Defining Areas of Performance

Not everyone who knows ISD is suited for the role of facilitating an analysis effort! I believe that the more varied the background and experiences that Analysts have (in their own job history or in other T&D analysis experiences), the easier they find the effort of defining Areas of Performance.

They can anticipate and stimulate the Analysis Team with

suggestions and straw models based on their ability to recognize patterns and similarities based on their past experiences.

Of course, if Analysts make suggestions time and again only to find that the Analysis Team doesn't buy it or doesn't quite buy it, they may find their own egos getting in the way of their success.

They may shut down and stop being the proactive facilitator the PACT Processes require. The timid shall not inherit the world of PACT.

The PACT Process facilitation almost always requires *driving* the process, not just *teeing up* the next step and then sitting back waiting for the Analysis Team to hand you the data!

Deficiencies of Environment, Knowledge and Skills, and Individual Attributes and Values

Three categories of deficiencies describe the probable barriers to superior performance. These are deficiencies of environmental supports (dE), of Knowledge and Skills (dK), and of individual attributes and values (dI).

Deficiency of Environmental Supports – dE

Environmental supports may be deficient and impede high performance. T&D cannot solve such deficiencies. T&D can only give the learner a heads-up that these are part of the imperfect world that they'll have to learn to deal with to be successful.

The dEs can include problems related to the following:

- Facilities
- Materials
- Methods and procedures
- Financial resources
- Consequence system
- Information and data
- Feedback
- Workload/timing

Deficiency of Knowledge and Skills – dK

Knowledge and skills of incumbent performers may be deficient, causing them to have difficulty performing the tasks required to produce the desired outputs at the appropriate quality standards.

T&D can usually solve these deficiencies unless a dI also exists.

Deficiency of Individual Attributes and Values – dI

T&D cannot solve deficiencies involving individual attributes and values; only a change in the selection system can affect these issues. (Appropriate T&D might be targeted at the managers or others responsible for recruiting, selecting, and hiring the target audience.)

The dIs can be caused by deficiencies in one or more of the individuals' attributes and values, including the following:

- Intellectual attributes
- Physical attributes
- Psychological attributes and values

Building the Performance Model

The Performance Model is built during the Analysis Team meeting by the Analyst and the Analysis Team.

They start by defining the Areas of Performance. Then for each Area of Performance, the group defines

- Performance outputs, key metrics/measures, and (sometimes) standards
- The tasks required to generate outputs
- The roles responsible for task performance
- Where the gaps are in performance
- The probable causes for those gaps, along with which of the three types of *deficiencies* are at work

During the model-building process, the Analyst may find it best to have internalized the questions shared in a couple of pages, and have ready two to three ways to phrase each one.

When I train others in these methods I do not allow them to use "my questions" – forcing them to find ways to paraphrase them – and thereby internalize them.

Conducting the Analysis Team Meeting

The Analysis Team Meeting is intended to produce the Performance Model and the Enabling Knowledge/Skill Matrices.

The formats you use to capture these two data-sets aren't critical, but capturing the data is.

Note that the Performance Model data is framed by first determining the Areas of Performance of the targeted performance, which is the equivalent of determining that ADDIE is the frame of an ISD professional's Performance Competence Requirements; or that DMAIC is for Six Sigma Professionals.

During the Analysis Team meeting, the Analyst and the Analysis Team members perform the process tasks listed below.

The Analyst explains the project background, the meeting objectives and process, the agenda, the outputs, and the roles and responsibilities of all present. While doing this, the Analyst responds to questions, comments, and concerns. The purpose of this task is to get everyone aligned prior to launching into the detailed analysis processes.

Then the Analyst and the Analysis Team launch into the real work by first determining those Areas of Performance – the segments of the work Performance Competence requirements.

For each Area of Performance, the group defines the performance outputs, their key metrics/measures, and (sometimes) standards. Then the group defines the tasks required to generate each outputs, and defines the roles responsible for task performance – using a coding system.

The group identifies gaps in performance along with the probable causes of those gaps. And for those causes, the group identifies which of the three types of *deficiency* categories are at work – using a coding system.

The Analyst then conducts a Process Check to ensure that everything the Analysis Team can think of (from task and output perspectives) are placed in one of the Areas of Performance data-sets.

The actions are then repeated for each Area of Performance.

Finally, the Analyst reviews what's been accomplished and previews the next analysis activities. Once the Performance Model is completed, it is used to systematically derive the discrete enabling Knowledge/Skill items by the predefined K/S Categories.

This is done through a review of each flip chart page mounted on the wall of the room – close enough for all to see AND read – one chart for each Area of Performance of the Performance Model.

The Analysis Team is led through this *very* systematic process to generate the list of Knowledge/Skill items. The Analyst must be able to facilitate the analysis process smoothly by owning and controlling the process, declaring ownership rights repeatedly but gently as necessary. Otherwise, the Analysis Team members may feel they can do the Analyst's job better by doing it differently.

If this happens, the Analyst loses control and may have a hard time regaining it. The resulting data deviations will have negative results in later analysis efforts and again in the Design Phase.

Of course, Analysts have to handle these proceedings carefully. They can't boast, "Hey, I own the darn process and I don't care what you Analysis Team members think or feel. I'm empowered here, now cooperate! Please!"

Rather, Analysts must articulate, with logical reasoning, why the process works the way it does and how the Performance

Model data fields are designed to smooth the transition from data gathering to downstream PACT design steps.

By definition, Master Performers are not dimwits, and logical reasoning should help the Analyst control the process.

Performance Model Data and Key Questions

Here are the questions the Analyst/facilitator poses to the Analysis Team to capture the AoPs and the Performance Competence Requirements on the Performance Model. See if you can paraphrase "my questions" for your eventual use.

Performance Data	Question(s) to Ask
Areas of Performance	• What are the major phases or elements of the performance or process? • What are the chunks of the job? • How can we break this performance up into some logical segments (somewhere between five to nine is ideal)?
Outputs Produced	• What are the key deliverables/outputs produced within this Area of Performance? • What is left over when you are finished performing the tasks?

Performance Data	Question(s) to Ask
Measures	• What are the measures/metrics that can be applied to the output? • How can you tell a good output from a bad one?
Standards	• What are the standards of acceptable performance given those measures?
Tasks Performed	• What are the tasks performed to produce those outputs?
Roles and Responsibilities	• Who is involved in this performance? For example, whose task responsibility is it to - E = Execute - S = Support - I = Input to - R = Review/give feedback - A = Approve/reject
Typical Performance Gaps	• Given those measures and standards, where do the performer's outputs typically fall short in meeting the expectations?

Additional Questions for the **Gap Analysis**:

Performance Data		Question(s) to Ask
Probable Gap Cause(s)	dE (Environment)	• Is the cause of the performance gap due to a lack of environmental supports? - Information/data - Organizational structure - Procedures/policies - Tools/equipment - Materials - Task interference - Feedback - Consequences
	dK (Knowledge/ Skill)	• Is the performance gap caused by a lack of the performer's knowledge and/or skill?
	dI (Individual Attribute/ Value)	• Is the performance gap caused by a poorly selected individual who has neither the physical, psychological, and/or intellectual attributes and/or values to perform or learn/acquire the skill?

The Performance Model describes on-the-job performance – both ideal and actual performance. Building a Performance

Model requires an interesting confluence of skills on the part of the Analyst, especially in defining Areas of Performance.

Based on the Performance Model, the Analyst is able to identify deficiencies in performance and to tell whether T&D is the appropriate way to address them. I've found it very helpful for the assigned Master Performers on the Analysis Team to see early that T&D isn't going to solve some (or maybe many) of the current performance deficiencies.

For deficiencies in Knowledge and Skills, the Knowledge/Skill Matrix is the way to start translating the identified deficiencies into prospective T&D.

Performance, Performance, Performance

Even if the T&D to be addressed is the seemingly "un-pin-down-able," nebulous, currently vogue topic of "Diversity Appreciation," there is a way to make it performance-based.

There is a business application for diversity – and appreciating it is hardly a first step. So the first thing to do is to declare our PACT intent. Call the product "Applying Diversity at the TMC Company" versus some form of appreciation.

Otherwise, why bother if we are not going to affect people's performance? Isn't that why we care about diversity in the first place, to affect people's behavior – and business results?

I believe there is always a performance context for all viable T&D. And if we can't pin that down, it's probably best to invest the shareholders' equity in something with a more tangible return – and not on appreciation type content.

About Knowledge/Skill Analysis

Identifying enabling, performance-based Knowledge and Skills is critical to the design and development of high-impact T&D. The systematic PACT Knowledge/Skill analysis effort follows immediately after the performance modeling effort.

The goal of Knowledge/Skill analysis is to derive systematically the enabling Knowledge/Skill (K/S) items and document them on Knowledge/Skill Matrices.

The K/S items documented are the enablers that lead to the ideal, high-performance state.

These are Knowledge/Skill items that are not just *thought* to be needed, but *known* to be needed.

The Knowledge/Skill Matrices link each Knowledge/Skill item to the performance that it enables (as described in the Performance Model).

Thus, the Performance Model ensures that the discrete Knowledge/Skill enablers in the Knowledge/Skill Matrices are performance relevant.

And, in turn, the performance orientation is passed on to the design work products for which the Knowledge/Skill Matrix is an input.

Knowledge/Skill Matrices

Knowledge/Skill Category: # ___ - _____   Page: ___ of ___

K/S Item	Link to Area of Performance							Select/ Train S/T	Criticality H/M/L	Difficulty H/M/L	Volatility H/M/L	Depth A/K/S
	A	B	C	D	E	F	G					

www.eppic.biz

To develop a Knowledge/Skill Matrix, the Knowledge/Skill items are identified AoP by AoP and listed on a matrix chart (see the example above).

The process uses a list of predefined Knowledge/Skill Categories, covered later in this chapter. Additional data points are gathered for each Knowledge/Skill item on the matrix; these are captured in the columns on the right-hand side of the matrix.

The data in the columns of the Knowledge/Skill Matrix is captured *live* by the facilitator during the same two- or three-day meeting in which the Performance Model is built.

Separating these two efforts is a terrible mistake – for so much is lost in terms of the data details by the Analysis Team in between sessions!!! The start-up time needed in that approach will require at least as much time as generating additional data. I've been forced to do this – and it just doesn't work well. Quality in terms of completeness and accuracy of the data suffers mightily.

K/S Matrices Data and Key Questions

Next – the questions for systematically deriving the Enabling Knowledge and Skill Matrices – based on the Performance Model data. Paraphrase "my questions" if you will.

Knowledge/Skill Data	Question(s) to Ask
Item	• What are the individual Knowledge/Skills under this category that are required to support any of the performance described in the Performance Model?
S/T: Select/Train	• Is this Knowledge/Skill item to be selected for when hiring a person or might it need to be trained for?
Link to Performance Model's AoPs	• The Knowledge/Skill item is required to support which of the Performance Model Areas of Performance?
Criticality	• How critical is this Knowledge/Skill to the overall performance? - High - Medium - Low

Knowledge/Skill Data	Question(s) to Ask

Learning Difficulty	• How difficult will it be for the learner to acquire this Knowledge/Skill?
	  - High
	  - Medium
	  - Low

Content Volatility	• This Knowledge/Skill item will require updating at a frequency of
	  - High
	  - Medium
	  - Low

Depth of Coverage Required	• How far must the training content go in addressing this Knowledge/Skill item?
	  - A = Awareness level
	  - K = Knowledge level
	  - S = Skill level

K/S Categories

A list (typically customized for each project) of predefined Knowledge/Skill categories allows the Analyst to control the brainstorming session. By structuring the brainstorming effort in this way, the Analyst can keep individual Knowledge/Skill items closely linked to performance as described in the Performance Model.

Not every category of K/S is needed for every MCD effort. I've reviewed these with the Project Steering Team in their first Gate Review Meeting – an advanced organizer for them to help them better anticipate the volume and organization of the data to be reviewed in their second GRM – and they sometimes down-select from the full list as they see fit.

And – I've also had Analysis Teams reverse that down-select of the PST and modify the list. But then, they were empowered by the PST to define both the Performance Competence Requirements and the Enabling K/Ss. So they did so.

The 17 Categories of K/S are:

1. Company Policies/Procedures/Practices/ Guidelines
2. Laws, Regulations, Codes, Agreements, and Contracts
3. Industry Standards
4. Internal Organizations and Resources
5. External Organizations and Resources
6. Marketplace Knowledge
7. Product/Service Knowledge
8. Process Knowledge
9. Records, Reports, Documents, and Forms
10. Materials and Supplies
11. Tools/Equipment/Machinery
12. Computer Systems/Software/Hardware
13. Personal/Interpersonal
14. Management/Supervisory
15. Business Knowledge and Skills
16. Professional/Technical
17. Functional Specific

The definitions for each of the 17 K/S categories follow.

Knowledge/Skill Category	Definition of the Knowledge/Skill Category
1 – Company Policies/ Procedures/ Practices/ Guidelines	Any rules the company expects employees to follow when performing their jobs.
2 – Laws, Regulations, Codes, Agreements, and Contracts	Laws or regulations from the government that basically govern the way you do your job. Any federal, state, or local laws or codes that drive our need to be compliant. Anything externally imposed that has the "power of the law" and would equate to jail time or fines if broken.
3 – Industry Standards	Industry-wide agreements that allow the TMC Company to be competitive. These are not imposed by regulatory agencies or policies and do not have the power of the law, but the power of the industry.

Knowledge/Skill Category	Definition of the Knowledge/Skill Category
4 – Internal Organizations and Resources	Internal departments, support groups, or other staff that help you accomplish work and/or are conduits to external entities.
5 – External Organizations and Resources	Outside agencies, companies, and professional or external sources you can use.
6 – Marketplace Knowledge	Industry-wide views regarding • Knowledge of Customers: types of Customers, specific companies, Customer types, the economic buyer or user of your product. • Knowledge of competitors: who are your competitors regarding a particular platform or product line. • Knowledge of competitive products: what are your competitive products?

Knowledge/Skill Category	Definition of the Knowledge/Skill Category
7 – Product/Service Knowledge	The products the Company produces or the services the Company provides. The company products or services that you need to know about to do your job. The depth you need will depend on the type of job you have.
8 – Process Knowledge	Formal or informal processes that cut across two or more organizations within the Company. If there is a policy or procedure covering this, then it need not be rewritten in this category.
9 – Records, Reports, Documents, and Forms	Any documents that you need to read, interpret, and/or complete.
10 – Materials and Supplies	The materials and supplies consumed in the performance of work.

Knowledge/Skill Category	Definition of the Knowledge/Skill Category
11 – Tools/ Equipment/ Machinery	Any tool or piece of equipment that you need to use. What classification of equipment might be needed? • Machinery: fixed and large • Equipment: movable and medium-sized • Tools: flexible and small
12 – Computer Systems/ Software/ Hardware	Any type of computer, peripheral, or particular software.
13 – Personal/ Interpersonal	Personal development knowledge or skills applicable to individual contributors.
14 – Management/ Supervisory	Knowledge or skills that are truly unique to a supervisor or manager that usually have legal implications.

Knowledge/Skill Category	Definition of the Knowledge/Skill Category
15 – Business Knowledge and Skills	Industry trends that equate to a business challenge. Any business challenges that become business strategies or business initiatives driven by business strategies.
16 – Professional/ Technical	Any knowledge particular to the profession being analyzed.
17 – Functional Specific	Any information that is specific to the functional area being studied.

The s*elect/train* column on the Matrices charts differentiates those K/S items that are attended to (if indeed they are) by the selection process, not the training process.

If the Knowledge/Skill item is supposed to be taken into account during the candidate selection process, the item should not be an issue for the T&D system. It won't be an issue if the selection system really screens for these enablers. However, if some people get the job without having the required enabler, there is a residual T&D implication to deal with.) The Analyst marks training items with a "T" and selection items with an "S."

The *criticality* column gives an assessment of the importance of the Knowledge/Skill item.

High level critical items should definitely be included in high-priority T&D Events in Modular Curriculum Development and Instructional Activity Development projects; low level criticality items may not.

The Analyst marks each item as H, M, or L (high, medium, or low criticality) as the Analysis Team dictates in response to the facilitated questions of the Analyst.

The *difficulty* column indicates how hard the Analysis Team assesses it will be for the target audience to grasp the awareness, knowledge, or skill related to this Knowledge/Skill item. The Analyst marks each item H, M, or L.

The *volatility* column is an assessment of the amount of maintenance required by the content covering the Knowledge/Skill item. Volatility impacts packaging and deployment/distribution strategies.

For example, an ISD professional might not want to put a volatile piece of content in e-learning and then have to update it quarterly – unless the distribution savings are so great that it would still be a good business decision to do so.

Also, later in the design process, it's a good idea to avoid placing volatile and nonvolatile content in the same T&D Lesson or Event; separating the two types of content reduces life-cycle maintenance costs for T&D products – depending on the exact media and mode of deployment. The Analyst marks this column H, M, or L.

The final column, *depth*, indicates the depth of coverage needed for the eventual/potential training to cover the

Knowledge/Skill item sufficiently for the learners to know how to apply it to performance.

 The Analyst and Analysis Team may decide that the appropriate depth is at the awareness level (A), the knowledge level (K), or the skill level (S). It should be clarified that marking these does not guarantee that this content will be addressed post-Analysis in the Design Phase. That's a decision for the PST – Project Steering Team.

How Detailed to Get?

As mentioned, the Knowledge/Skill Matrix lists Knowledge/Skill items and links them back to the Performance Model. Usually this linkage is made at the Area of Performance level, but it could be at the output or task level. Outputs and tasks are listed for each Area of Performance in a Performance Model.

Some of my Clients thought it necessary and more useful to link each Knowledge/Skill item to the Role for each task. Again, I usually link to the Area of Performance during Analysis and later will use the Design Team members' knowledge of the more detailed linkages during the design process to accomplish what this more detailed effort would have accomplished earlier.

My approach saves time, avoids analysis paralysis and accomplishes the same result – but more effectively – as all of those more detailed will be scrutinized all over again doing double duty on each) later.

I've been there and done that – and understand how that plays out; most of my clients don't see that coming – and therefore insist on a more detailed linking exercise. I add the extra time to the Project Plan (having addressed this back in

Phase 1) as it extends these Analysis Meetings to about double the time required – along with the team size, ability/willingness to come to consensus, etc.

In PACT, we like to defer the details until just when they are needed. The increased cycle time required to link at a lower level may add a day or two - depending on the amount of data generated during the analysis process.

And that both smells and feels like analysis paralysis! So I avoid it where and when possible.

Conducting the Knowledge/Skill Analysis Effort with the Analysis Team

To accomplish the Knowledge/Skill Analysis, the Analyst and the Analysis Team perform six tasks.

First, the Analysis Team reviews the Knowledge/Skill category list and modifies it if necessary. The team needs to understand the definitions of each category and how to deal with the inevitable overlaps between categories. Have them give you examples that you'll list later – just to prime their mental pumps!

Second, taking a single Knowledge/Skill category at a time, the Analysis Team reviews each Area of Performance from the Performance Model. All enabling Knowledge/Skill items that the Analysis Team can think of/derive from that review of the Outputs, Tasks, etc. are listed.

This is highly structured brainstorming. The Knowledge/Skill categories are used to focus on types of Knowledge/Skills, and the Performance Model charts are used to focus and stimulate the thinking of the team.

Third, the team links each Knowledge/Skill item to all appropriate Areas of Performance.

Fourth, after each Knowledge/Skill Category has been addressed, the Analyst returns to the first Knowledge/Skill Matrix and completes all of the remaining columns in the order below.

- Starting with the s*elect/train* column, each Knowledge/Skill item is evaluated to determine if an employee will be screened out if he or she does not possess the Knowledge/Skill (S) in the selection process, or if training will need to be provided (T). (Note that the selection process must absolutely screen, for if it doesn't, you'll eventually confront a T&D issue. If you're not sure, it gets a "T".)
- Then the *criticality to performance* is rated high, medium, or low.
- The *difficulty to learn* is rated high, medium, or low.
- The *volatility of content* of the Knowledge/Skill item is rated high, medium, or low.
- The *level of depth* that any T&D should go to is defined as awareness, knowledge, or skill.

Once the Performance Model and K/S Matrices data is captured, the Analysis Team should be debriefed.

Analysis Team Meeting Debriefing

The Debriefing Steps
When it's time to debrief, debrief quickly, but not too briefly.

Make sure the team has had a recent break. Offer them a five- or ten-minute break before starting the debrief. Let them know that the debriefing may take 20 to 40 minutes.

This debriefing happens at the conclusion of a 2-3-4 day meeting – for both the Analysis Team Meeting and again for the Design Team Meeting. Note: sometimes these analysis and design efforts are combined – and the debriefing is modified appropriately.

Note: a typical cycle time for both the Analysis Team Meeting and the Design Team Meeting is 3 days each – where we move quickly through the structured process – gathering consensus data at each step at "the level of depth" needed for the next downstream step.

This is where many members of the team might struggle.

They might have expected us to "boil the ocean to get a cup of tea" – and detail everything right here in this meeting – including designing and developing the content. The process doesn't do that up front – as many things found/uncovered perhaps won't be deemed critical enough to warrant investments in training – being left then to Un-Structured OJT, also known today as Informal Learning.

And we didn't need or want the extreme depth/detail to simply enable the Customer and Stakeholders to make the business decisions as "what to continue with to address with investments" of effort, time and money – and what to drop right away – where they don't see enough R of the I (as in ROI).

And – we avoid analysis paralysis.

The debriefing for the Analysis Team is focused around these five questions.

1. What percent of everything under the "sun and moon" did we capture in terms of our coverage of the outputs, tasks, and enabling Knowledge and Skills within our project's scope?

2. What percent of *everything critical*, and not *just necessary*, did we capture in terms of our coverage of the outputs, tasks, and enabling Knowledge and Skills within our project's scope?

3. What did you personally think of the product we produced? The *content* of both the Performance Model *charts* and the Knowledge/Skill Matrices *charts*?

4. What did you think of the *process* we employed to produce the Performance Model *charts* and the Knowledge/Skill Matrices *charts*?

5. What do you see as the *key issues going forward* for our Project Steering Team to address?

I go to the flip chart and on a blank page I frame my first two questions so that everyone can read my words rather than try to remember what I said as we do a systematic round-robin.

Remember . . . always try to make it visible.

What % of "**everything under the sun and moon**" did we capture in terms of our coverage of the outputs, tasks, and enabling Knowledge and Skills within our project's scope?	What % of "**everything critical**," and not just necessary, did we capture in terms of our coverage of the outputs, tasks, and enabling Knowledge and Skills within our project's scope?

I ask them to each write their answers to these first two questions down on any piece of paper in front of them – and then I gather them all up – and write their responses onto the flip chart page.

Too often I have sensed that members who did not write down their answers changed them as we went around the table asking others for their numbers. Peer pressure among Master Performers? Yes, there too.

I also insist prior to starting this debriefing that the team members not be interrogated by the others in the room about their answers – as I believe: it is what it is.

But in truth I often lose control here – and they do it anyway. So I usually let them – unless someone interjects my stated "rule" to help fend off those with inquiring minds.

I capture all of the answers to the other three questions on a flip chart easel so that all may see exactly what I write down so that they can edit before we end the meeting.

I then remind them of the next steps in the Analysis Phase. Then we end the meeting and I send them off back to their day jobs.

They are typically mentally exhausted/ drained – and need to recharge – before we meet again.

Existing T&D Assessment

The intent of assessing existing T&D is to salvage, as appropriate, all of the previous T&D that meets the needs articulated and captured in the analysis meeting.

The goal is to avoid reinventing T&D that is already in place. Effectively conducting this portion of the analysis effort saves organizational resources by recycling reusable T&D either "as is" or "after modification" – as appropriate for our needs for authentic content.

After analyzing performance requirements and Knowledge/Skill enablers, existing T&D can be assessed for its fit within the architecture designed by CAD - Curriculum Architecture Design, MCD - Modular Curriculum Development, or IAD - Instructional Activity Development.

The PACT analysis process by which this happens is called the Existing T&D Assessment (ETA).

The goals of the Existing T&D Assessment are to

- Reuse everything in the T&D inventory that fits, using the T&D as is in the new Curriculum Architecture Design, Modular Curriculum Development, or Instructional Activity Development project.
- Identify what to fix if the T&D doesn't quite fit; the T&D will need to be modified/updated for use in the CAD, MCD, or IAD products.
- Don't use the T&D that doesn't fit - at least for the audiences we are analyzing; the existing T&D will

not be used at all for our needs – but may be OK for other audiences.

The Performance Model and Knowledge/Skill Matrix provided a "bill of materials" for the content of the ideal, blue sky CAD - Curriculum Architecture Design, or for a piece of a curriculum being addressed in an MCD or IAD effort.

They also provide a set of shopping criteria to be used to assess existing T&D. The criteria can also be used to procure T&D in the marketplace.

The Performance Model and Knowledge/Skill Matrix are used to investigate and assess any instruction and information currently in the organization's T&D inventory.

In some instances, content from outside the organization is assessed. That takes a lot longer – and should have been decided back in the Phase 1 efforts – before the plan and schedule were locked into.

Using the Performance Model and the Knowledge/Skill Matrix means that this assessment of existing content is also grounded in data about Performance Competence, not simply opinion based on face-validity.

Who Does What During an ETA
The key players in the Existing T&D Assessment are the PACT Analyst (or the PACT Project Manager) along with representatives from the T&D supplier organizations.

The Analyst is usually the best person to represent the PACT side of things, unless the Project Manager was in the analysis meeting and understands the data in the Performance Model and Knowledge/Skill Matrix.

Each T&D supplier is given the chance to nominate various training and development products as being appropriate to the needs identified and captured in the Performance Model and the Knowledge/Skill Matrices.

Inputs and Likely Sources for the Existing T&D Assessment

Key inputs may come from existing course catalogs or from ISD personnel knowledgeable about the company's T&D.

It is sometimes a difficult task to gather all of the T&D and find the right people to speak for the T&D that may be applicable to the project's needs.

The Analyst can speed the effort by contacting likely sources prior to conducting the Existing T&D Assessment and forewarning them by describing the analysis process, the information needed, and when it will be needed.

Tasks Performed during an Existing T&D Assessment

The tasks performed during an Existing T&D Assessment effort are generally performed by the Analyst, although in some cases the Project Manager may do them.

First, the Analyst contacts the likely sources of T&D prior to the assessment. The sources may include outside vendors of T&D, but most often this effort is limited to internal sources. In a large company, this can be quite an effort; the team should not underestimate the task's cycle time or the number of hours the task may take.

Once the Analyst has documented the Performance Model and Knowledge/Skill Matrix data, advance copies can be sent to the T&D suppliers. The Analyst needs to be sure the suppliers understand the format of these analysis outputs and how to interpret the data on them.

When meeting with the T&D suppliers, the Analyst reviews the courses and other T&D that the suppliers believe meet the needs documented. Then the Analyst fills out the Existing T&D Assessment forms.

Finally, the Analyst includes the Existing T&D Assessment data in the Analysis Report and in the presentation for the Project Steering Team Gate Review Meeting.

This meeting occurs after Phase 2 in Curriculum Architecture Design, Modular Curriculum Development, and Instructional Activity Development.

Documenting the Analysis Outputs

The Analysis Report documents all of the analysis data from the Analysis Phase of PACT.

Analysis Reports vary in formality, depending on the culture of the organization and the need to document this data for future reference. Is the data looked upon as simply a means to an end or as an end point in-and-of-itself?

There are many advantages to being formal and detailed; this helps satisfy those who want details and those who will follow up later, maybe months or years later, using the data to create T&D.

It's beneficial to create and circulate a *full* Analysis Report rather than simply a summary of the analysis meeting outputs.

The full document provides a context for the analysis meeting outputs. It provides the background of the project, tells that there are other phases following the Analysis Phase, describes who is on the Project Steering Team, and so forth.

All of this information is useful to anyone who happens to receive the Analysis Report without knowing the history of the project.

In addition, the detailed material in the full Analysis Report provides support for discussions during the Project Steering Team meeting that takes place as a gate review for the Analysis Phase.

It's useful to orient Project Steering Team members to the nature of the analysis outputs *before* describing them in detail. For example, this means explaining the nature of Areas of Performance and how they relate to outputs and tasks. Similarly, it's useful to explain Knowledge/Skill Categories before reviewing the details of the Knowledge/Skill Matrices.

The Project Manager or Analyst can generally move fairly quickly through the points in the Project Steering Team presentation, using appropriate media to focus reviewers on points of discussion. Project Steering Team members will slow the presentation down when they want to ask questions or discuss items and issues in more detail.

Two things help the Analyst move quickly through the presentation. First, Analysis Team members are handpicked by the Project Steering Team for competence and credibility; this tends to "pre-bless" the outputs reviewed during this meeting. Second, most Project Steering Team members may be in positions where they no longer feel the need to manage at the micro-level of detail for these details.

With a Little Help from My Friends

Analysis Team members can help accomplish the goals of this Project Steering Team meeting in two ways. First, I encourage Analysis Team members to tell their Project

Steering Team sponsors before the review meeting how things went during the analysis effort.

Usually what they say is something along the lines of, "I hated the process but loved the product." So Project Steering Team members have advance information that the analysis meeting went well.

Second, sometimes Analysis Team members show up at the Project Steering Team meeting. The message they send to the Project Steering Team—subtly or not-so-subtly—is, "We're here representing the Analysis Team.

We want to make sure you don't mess up what we accomplished in that analysis meeting." Usually the Project Steering Team gets the point.

When the Project Steering Team members are finished with their questions and comments, the Analyst or Project Manager can bring up analysis issues, lobby for Design Team members, and preview the remainder of the project.

Once the Project Steering Team has reviewed, modified, sanctioned, and approved the analysis data, the PACT project moves into its next phase. There, armed with the insights gained from the collection and organization of the analysis data, the project can proceed smoothly into the design efforts appropriate for the project.

Project Management Considerations for PACT Analysis

Several Project Management considerations are specific to the Analysis Phase. One consideration is planning the amount of time required to perform the existing T&D analysis.

Examination of existing T&D is done after the Analysis Team Meeting. The goal is to use existing T&D where possible in order to save organizational resources.

For the Project Manager, the tradeoff is between the time and effort required to find and assess all relevant existing T&D versus the cost to re-create some T&D unnecessarily.

In a large organization where T&D is widely dispersed, a fair amount of time and money might be required to do a complete Existing T&D Assessment.

Another consideration is the length of the Analysis Phase Gate Review Meeting. The meeting must be long enough to raise *and* resolve project issues; proceeding without resolution guarantees later rework.

The Gate Review Meeting during the Analysis Phase is one day – just under one third of a Project Steering Team member's total commitment to an MCD effort.

If the Project Manager encounters resistance to the commitment of a day during this phase, the comeback is: If this project is not worth a day of your time now and three and a half days altogether, then perhaps we are not designing and developing the high-impact, high-payoff T&D we thought we were, and perhaps this project is not worthwhile.

As project Stakeholders, that's their decision.

The size and amount of detail in the Analysis Report should also be considered.

As mentioned earlier, it's recommended that the Project Manager avoid distributing summary documents, because without the background information in the full Analysis Report, a summary lacks context and other vital information.

For Project Steering Team members who seem to have a problem with the entire document, the Project Manager can recommend delegating review of the Analysis Report to a trusted subordinate.

Chapter Summary & Transition

This chapter was intended to provide you details about Phase 2 of an MCD effort: Analysis.

The outputs of the four PACT analytic methods described in this section of the book are inputs to later phases of the PACT Processes.

The methods ensure that the training developed later is performance-based. This chapter describes the final steps necessary in Analysis before moving on to those other phases.

PACT Analysis Summary

The four key analytic methods used in Phase 2 of the PACT Processes are:

- Analyzing Target Audience Data
- Performance Modeling
- Knowledge/Skill Analysis
- Existing T&D Assessment

These four are the primary, but not the exclusive, types of analyses that happen within PACT MCD projects.

This chapter flows logically into the next, on Phase 3, however your needs may cause you to want to skip around.

The following are the chapter titles and page numbers to assist you with your personal navigation needs.

Suggested Chapter Reflection & Reaction

I would suggest that prior to jumping into whichever chapter meets your needs that you give pause for a moment to reflect on the following and make some notes:

- Does this have applicability for me?

- What can I adopt from what I have read here?

- What are my potential needs for adaptation?

- What other issues do I see that I will need to address before embracing?

Please make note of your thoughts before proceeding.

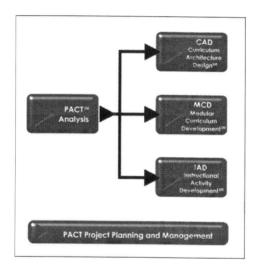

3 levels of ISD Methodologies
with common Analysis and
Project Planning & Management Methodologies.

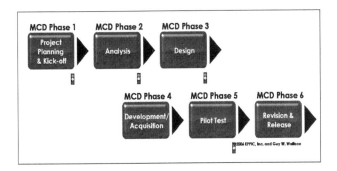

8 – PHASE 3: DESIGN

Chapter Overview

This chapter is intended to provide you details about the MCD Design phase.

Warning: there is a lot here to cover.

MCD Phase 3: Design

During the third phase of Modular Curriculum Development, Design, modules are designed at a level appropriate to the project's scope.

With the Design Team's assistance, Event Specs and Maps are produced. The Maps are visually sequenced versions of the Specs.

The Event Specs and Maps are further refined into Lesson Specs and Maps, and then into Activity Specs - the last level of design detail of the PACT Processes.

All Phase 3 outputs are captured and reported out in a Design Document and a presentation for the PST – Project Steering Team. The design and presentation are reviewed for approval and/or revisions by the Project Steering Team during their 3rd Gate Review Meeting at the end of this phase.

Overview of MCD Phase 3: Design

Description – In this phase, the Design Team is facilitated through a systematic design process during a meeting. After the meeting, additional design details are completed by the ISD Team and then everything is reviewed by the Project Steering Team.

Key Activities/Tasks – A multi-day Design Team meeting is held, typically with several members from the Analysis Team if not all of them. They are facilitated to produce the Modular Curriculum Development design outputs using the Analysis data as inputs for actual/eventual content – or to influence the content design.

The ISD Team details the design and documents it all. Finally, a Project Steering Team Gate Review Meeting is held to review and approve the design – or to modify it. Modifications are made, if necessary post GRM and used in the next Phase. The Project Steering Team also discusses and plans the Pilot-Test – as they can now more easily imagine the content's configuration and its media and modes.

Key Outputs – The key output of this phase is a Design Document that includes:

- Event Specifications
- Event Map of Lessons
- Lesson Specifications
- Lesson Maps of Activities
- Instructional Activity Specifications

Note: The intent of the team approach to design is *not* to design by committee - but to *influence* the Designers by committee during the actual design activities.

The tasks of Phase 3 for Modular Curriculum Development are organized into four sub-phases.

MCD Subphase 3.1 – Predesign Planning, Data Gathering, and Preparation

The purpose of this sub-phase is to prepare any new players for their participation in the remainder of the Modular Curriculum Development project. For example, the ISD Designer may be new to the project and different than the Analyst or Project Manager. During this sub-phase, the Designer prepares for the Design Team meeting by getting the analysis data into shape for use in the design process.

MCD Subphase 3.2 – Design Process and Documentation

Included in this sub-phase are the design meeting itself and post-meeting design documentation activities. Work includes preparing for the Design Team meeting, conducting the meeting to design the T&D, and documenting the design work products. In addition, the Designer and Project Manager prepare for the Gate Review Meeting in Subphase 3.3.

MCD Subphase 3.3 – Phase 3 Gate Review

During this sub-phase, the Project Steering Team participates in a design review. Activities in this sub-phase include preparations for the Gate Review Meeting and the meeting itself.

Just as with analysis data, design details are often too voluminous for a line-by-line review in the allotted time. It is up to the Modular Curriculum Development Project Manager and Designer to facilitate the Project Steering Team through a review that hits the highlights and brings out any problem areas.

Problems can arise due to Design Team consensus issues, instructional integrity issues, insights from the ISD practitioners, etc.

Now is the time to face the issues squarely and get them resolved before they wind up as the next pile of rework.

MCD Subphase 3.4 – Phase 3 Completion and Transition

In this sub-phase, the design is updated based on the Project Steering Team feedback and directives. Formal sign-offs are obtained as required in the organizational setting. Then the project is ready to move into the Development Phase of Modular Curriculum Development.

More Task Detail for MCD Phase 3: Design

Scan these detailed Task Listings for now – organized by the four sub-phases of Phase 3: Design, to simply become somewhat familiar with what's got to be done in this part of an MCD effort.

You will probably need to adapt this detailed listing – rather than adopt it for your context – when you are planning your first real project.

MCD Subphase 3.1 – Predesign Planning, Data Gathering, and Preparation

1. The Project Manager reviews the project with the newly assigned Designer (as needed), and provides all resource materials for the Designer's orientation.

2. The Designer reviews the Project Plan, the Analysis Report, and all other resource and background materials provided. The Designer obtains additional materials and clarifies issues (via phone or in person) as needed.

3. The Designer coordinates logistics for any individual interviews required before the design meeting. The Designer contacts all participants and informs them about the project, purpose, outputs, process, and their specific roles. The Designer selects meeting methods, locations, dates, and times.

4. The Designer prepares for predesign interviews and meetings, determining what information to gather, verify, and discuss. The Designer uses the information

to develop the predesign agenda. This information may include

- Reactions from the Project Steering Team analysis Gate Review Meeting and implications for the design meeting
- Concepts related to the CAD, to MCD, or to T&D Events/Modules; these concepts might include
  - Overall cycle time and incurred time constraints for curriculum deployment
  - Additions and changes to deployment platforms from the CAD design (if appropriate)
  - Criteria for the MCD, for example
    - Roles, responsibilities, and definitions for deployment strategies (structured, on-the-job training; group-paced classroom training; group-paced lab training; E-LEARNING; etc.)
    - Timing and event time issues
    - Training sites
    - Considerations for the MCD
      1. Existing T&D Assessments and their use
      2. Specific political or supply-chain issues

5. The Designer conducts predesign interviews and meetings.
6. The Designer uses PACT templates to develop initial design straw models. These models are to be used to jump-start the design process. The Designer may, as appropriate, prepare models of
   - Event Specs and Maps (blanks)
   - Lesson Specs and Maps (blanks)
   - Instructional Activity Specs (blanks)
   - Knowledge/Skill Slip-sheets (completed with all Knowledge/Skill items from the Knowledge/Skill Matrices)

- Existing T&D Assessment Sheets from the Analysis Phase
7. The Designer reviews all design straw models with designated ISD organization staff members prior to the use of the straw models in the design process. This is to ensure that all of the event's module content configuration conforms to the ISD organization's modularity rules and guidelines. The Designer is to re-modularize the models as needed.

MCD Subphase 3.2 – Design Process and Documentation

1. The Project Manager coordinates all logistics for the Phase 3 Design Team meeting, including
   - Meeting method, location, dates, and times
   - Arrangements for meeting materials, equipment, and food and beverage
   - Invitations and communications about
     - Date, time, location, and directions
     - Accommodations for travel, living, meals, etc.
     - The project, meeting purpose, outputs, process, specific roles, and any preparations required on the part of meeting participants
2. The Project Manager confirms attendance of all key participants and completion of all assigned prework immediately prior to the design meeting.
3. The Designer and Project Manager prepare all meeting materials and orient any additional project staff participants for the upcoming Design Team meeting. The following are prepared, as appropriate:
   - Agendas
   - Assignments
   - Briefings

4. The Designer conducts the design process using either a multiday Design Team meeting or meetings with individual Design Team members. The Designer
   - Orients the team to the project and the meeting
   - Uses blank templates or straw models to create the following:
     - Event Specs and Event Maps of Lessons
     - Lesson Specs and Lesson Maps of Activities
     - Instructional Activity Specs
   - Completes the MCD outputs, including
     - Assessing the work of the team and identifying any open issues for the Project Steering Team to address
     - Closing the meeting and the design process
5. The Designer documents the design process outputs using templates and go-by's.
6. The Designer documents the design meeting outputs and all other post-design process outputs. The Designer adds "content"; the use of exact wording from the Performance Model and Knowledge/Skill Matrix is ideal. The Designer copies from the model and matrix onto the T&D Module Spec the following items:
   - Area of Performance outputs, tasks, and roles
   - Knowledge/skill items
   - Anything and everything else that reasonably fits to explain the T&D Event content (while the Designer may add as he or she sees fit, it may be handy at this point to check with the team to help remember the words that didn't make it onto the meeting flip charts)
7. The Designer conducts additional, detailed assessments of any and all existing T&D programs and materials, as appropriate. This is done via searches in the ISD organization's T&D databases, examination of

paper files, checks of libraries, and discussions with key ISD organization personnel. The Designer documents the updates using the Existing T&D Assessment templates. In discussion with ISD personnel, the Designer determines whether and where to look for the potential procurement of already-built T&D materials from outside the organization.

8. The Designer meets with ISD management and, if appropriate, updates the
   - Development/Acquisition Strategy and Plan
   - Deployment Strategy and Plan
   - Evaluation Strategy and Plan
9. The Designer develops the MCD Design Document using templates and go-by's.
10. The Designer produces and forwards copies of the Design Document and Project Steering Team gate review presentation to T&D organization management for their preview before the Gate Review Meeting.

MCD Subphase 3.3 – Phase 3 Gate Review

1. The Project Manager coordinates all logistics for the Phase 3 Project Steering Team Gate Review Meeting, including
   - Meeting method, location, dates, and times
   - Arrangements for meeting materials, equipment, and food and beverage
   - Invitations and communications about
     - Date, time, location, and directions
     - Accommodations for travel, living, meals, etc.
     - The project, meeting purpose, outputs, process, specific roles, and any preparations required on the part of meeting participants
2. The Project Manager confirms attendance of all key participants and completion of all assigned prework

immediately prior to the Project Steering Team meeting.

3.   The Project Manager prepares meeting materials and prepares participants for the meeting. Preparations include

- Agendas
- Gate review presentation materials and all handout materials
- Assignments
- Briefings

4.   The Project Manager conducts an eight-hour Phase 3 Project Steering Team Gate Review Meeting to

- Review the MCD project purpose, business drivers, approach, process, deliverables, and schedule for key milestones.
- Review all actuals compared to plan, the rationale for all deviations, and the effect of deviations on the project's cost and schedule performance.
- Review the MCD design specifics, including the
  - Event Spec and Event Map of Lessons
  - Lesson Specs and Lesson Maps of Activities
  - Instructional Activity Specs
- Review non-training issues.
- Identify all other key project issues (problems, opportunities, goals, constraints, etc.).
- Discuss the current
  - Development/Acquisition Strategy and Plan
  - Deployment Strategy and Plan
  - Evaluation Strategy and Plan
- Identify a lead Subject Matter Expert/Master Performer (SME/MP) for resolving any and all developmental issues that arise during the development/acquisition efforts.

- Assess the phase completion status using the Phase 3 exit criteria—for example, have outputs been approved.

MCD Subphase 3.4 – Phase 3 Completion and Transition

1. The Project Manager determines any changes required to the Modular Curriculum Development Design Document and the Project Plan/Proposal, and resolves any staffing issues for the next phase.
2. The Project Manager and Designer update the Design Document and Project Plan/Proposal (as needed) based on the Project Steering Team meeting and decisions. The documents are forwarded to all appropriate project participants and key Stakeholders.
3. The Project Manager obtains sign-offs from ISD management and from the Customer, the Project Steering Team chairperson.
4. The Project Manager gathers all project resource materials, holding them for use by the assigned developers.

The Design Team Meeting

The Analysis Team meeting lays the groundwork for the design, but the Design Team meeting is the heart of any good Modular Curriculum Development project. From it comes a design for performance-based T&D.

Overview

The purpose of the Design Team meeting is to use the Design Team's input to develop specifications and maps for T&D Events, Lessons, and Activities.

The meeting facilitator guides this process. All in all, these outputs provide reviewers with what they need to evaluate the design, and they provide developers with what they need to build the T&D.

Using a meeting for design helps hold down costs and cycle time, keeping the process lean and accelerated.

Input from various members of the Design Team keeps the process Customer-driven. And while ISD'ers own the process, Customers own the content and the results.

The length of the Design Team meeting depends on the scope of the project, but a typical meeting lasts two to four days.

The Design Team

In keeping with the establishment of a "pact" with ISD's constituencies, the design process uses a Design Team to guide and react to the design elements and the activity flow within each lesson, each module, and each event. The Design Team consists of just a few individuals representing the following groups:

- Master Performers
- Subject Matter Experts
- Managers and Supervisors

During the meeting, these team members are joined by the ISD Designer and the Project Manager.

The Design Team should be limited to members from the Analysis Team to ensure continuity and a quicker start-up. New players have a steep learning curve to climb, and that will usually have a negative impact on meeting and project cycle times and costs. New players should rarely be admitted, and if they are, extensive briefings must take place before the Design Team meeting.

Design Team members must have credibility with the Project Steering Team, or else the Project Steering Team will later "micro-critique" the design and rework it, decreasing the benefits of the team approach.

In the meeting, the Design Team's continuous communication with the ISD tends to reduce the overall design cycle time and enhance the design's quality.

The Designer

With the Design Team, the Designer's job includes facilitating and controlling the team members and the instructional design process—managing the normal conflicts and varied opinions, ensuring that sound instructional strategies and methods are employed, and so forth.

While the Designer's job is a bit more difficult upfront, the back-end product is worth the front-end trouble; furthermore, the team approach minimizes potential downstream design rework.

Creating the detailed training design using the Design Team as a sounding board is a challenge for the ISD Designer. Instructional design theories, approaches, and previous lessons learned must be communicated to the team.

Designers can't expect the team to buy all of their instructional theories and rules automatically; these must be *sold*. And if the theories and rules don't make sense to the team, they may need to be modified to fit reality as the other team members see it.

Most importantly, unless a Designer has a reputation within the Design Team as a great instructional Designer, he or she has to *earn* those stripes during the design process.

The Designer cannot expect the team to defer to his/her superior wisdom and educational background just because he or she thinks they should. They might, but usually only when they feel the Designer *deserves* that deference.

The Designer must prove his or her worthiness, and that will most likely come from demonstrated competence, flexibility, and openness to the teams' ideas.

The Challenge of Design

Designers can let their own egos get in the way. It can be quite difficult to find yourself being constantly challenged regarding your design concepts and details. And here you are, constantly asking for it! This is the dilemma of team design.

Again, we don't subscribe to the notion of designing by committee; rather, we like to think of it as influencing the Designer by committee.

Preparing for the MCD Design Meeting

Preparing for the Modular Curriculum Development design meeting involves

- Coordinating the logistics for the design meeting
- Reviewing project outputs generated so far
- Developing "straw dog" models as guides for many of the potential outputs from the design meeting
- Creating the materials needed for the design meeting

process

Outputs from this preparation could include

- The blank formats and templates for use within the design process
- The straw model MCD design elements; these may be some (but not all) of the following:
  - Knowledge/Skill Slipsheets
  - Blank T&D Event Specs and Maps
  - Blank Lesson Specs and Maps
  - Completed Existing T&D Assessment forms
  - Copies of the Performance Model and Knowledge/Skill Matrix for use by the Design Team members

As part of the preparation for the Design Team meeting, the meeting facilitator (the Project Manager or the ISD Designer) has certain specific tasks to perform. For example, the facilitator must

- Review any requirements and constraints imposed on the design effort from the Project Steering Team or the ISD organization. These may include requirements for
  - Formats
  - Naming conventions
  - Types of T&D methods to be used or avoided
  - Determine the outputs to be produced in the Modular Curriculum Development design meeting, given the project's scope and deliverables.
- For example, how many Events will be designed and for whom?
  - What are the Events design formats and templates to be used, and what restrictions exist for changing them?

- Update the forms and templates as needed and produce them in the quantities needed.
- As an exercise, practice beginning the design process. This helps raise the Designer's comfort level with getting the Design Team up and running.
- Clean up everything, and get it organized for use in the real design process at the design meeting.

Conducting the MCD Design Meeting

In the design meeting, the facilitator creates a consensus regarding the T&D design outputs.

If the ISD Designer has built straw dog models of various design outputs, he or she may wish to use them as a jump-starter for the team; alternatively, the Designer may wish to use them only in case the meeting bogs down.

Modular Curriculum Development design meeting steps are listed below. The facilitator's role in each of these steps is then explained in more detail.

- Orient the Design Team to the project, process, and outputs, as needed.
- Create or review a list of MCD design concepts, criteria, and constraints.
- Map the Events' Lessons, adhering to the rules of modularity and sort the Analysis data into each Lesson; adding data as needed.
- Map the Lessons' Instructional Activities and resort the analysis data; adding data as needed.
- Spec out some or all of the Instructional Activities (this may or may not happen during the design meeting; more typically it happens partially).
- Debrief the Design Team, review the next steps of the project, and close the meeting.

First, the facilitator familiarizes the team with the project's intent, drivers, focus, and limitations. He or she gives an overview of the process, reviewing the tasks to be performed, the outputs to be generated, the rough time frames for the meeting process, etc.

Then comes an explanation of team roles and the facilitator's role: team members own the content; ISD owns the process. In addition, the facilitator manages the team's expectations and establishes the facilitator's control and ownership of the process – while establish the Team's role and ownership in the what, when and how deep of the content to be covered.

Second, the facilitator creates or reviews a list of MCD design concepts, criteria, and constraints. This step makes the Stakeholders' expectations and measures visible to all involved in the design process.

A list of concepts and criteria, along with important considerations such as maximum course length, is created to reflect the desires and needs of the target audiences, their management, and the training organization.

Also, the Design Team notes concepts about the future training system and the criteria Customers will use for evaluating the eventual outputs of the project. Some training Customers, for example, may reject courses less than five days in length.

This list of concepts and criteria will provide guidance in developing the Event or Events and the Lessons that constitute each Event.

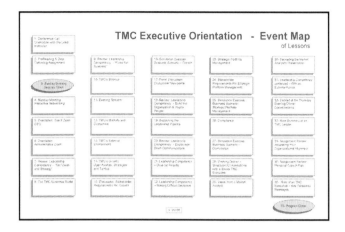

Third, the facilitator creates visual map of the Lessons in the T&D Events and generates a Lesson Map and a Lesson Spec – for each Lesson on the Event Map.

The Lesson Specs lead to the Instructional Activity Spec - which contains all of the content from the analysis data – in the final sort and processing of that analysis data.

An example Lesson Map follows.

Guy W. Wallace

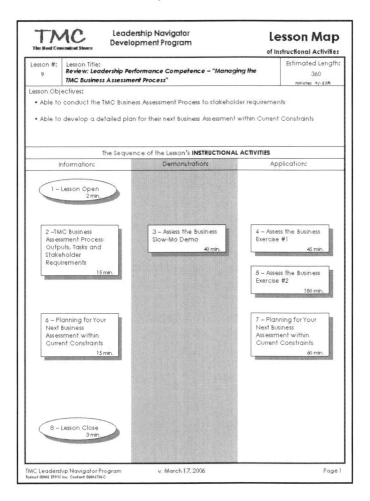

Next, the facilitator details the T&D Instructional Activity
Specs (which are most often completed *after* the Design
Team meeting by the ISD Designers).

178

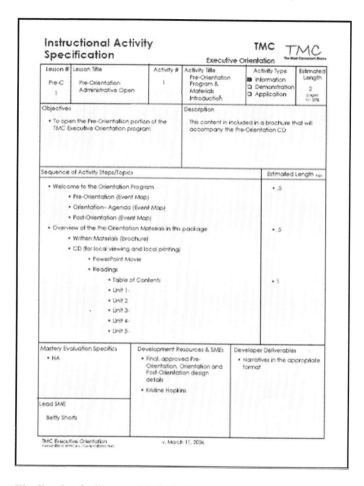

Finally, the facilitator debriefs the Design Team, reviews the next steps, and closes the Design Team meeting.

To do this, he or she

- Assesses the meeting's success: the process and the products produced
- Identifies any leftover issues for the Project Steering Team

- Thanks everyone and closes the meeting

Design Team Meeting Debriefing

The Debriefing Steps
Again, this debriefing happens at the conclusion of a 2-3-4 day Design Team Meeting.

The debriefing for the Design Team is focused around these five questions.

1. What percent of everything under the "sun and moon" did we capture in our L&D/ T&D Event and Lesson Maps and Specifications for the Target Audiences within our project's scope?

2. What percent of *everything critical*, and not *just necessary*, did we capture in our L&D/ T&D Event and Lesson Maps and Specifications for the Target Audiences within our project's scope?

3. What did you personally think of the product we produced? The *content* of the L&D/ T&D Path(s) and the Event and Module Specifications for the Target Audiences' Path?

4. What did you think of the *process* we employed to produce the Event and Lesson Maps and Specifications for the Target Audiences?

5. What do you see as the *key issues going forward* for our Project Steering Team to address?

I go to the flip chart and on a blank page I frame my first two questions so that everyone can read my words rather than try to remember what I said as we do a systematic round-robin.

Remember . . . always try to make it visible.

What % of "**everything under the sun and moon**" did we capture in our L&D/ T&D Event and Lesson Maps & Specifications for the Target Audiences within our project's scope?	What % of "**everything critical**," and not just necessary, did we capture in our L&D/ T&D Event and Lesson Maps & Specifications for the Target Audiences within our project's scope?

Again, I ask them to each write their answers to these first two questions down on any piece of paper in front of them – and then I gather them all up – and write their responses onto the flip chart page.

Then I capture their responses as close to verbatim as I can, on the flip chart pages in full view of everyone – and let them edit/correct what I don't capture quite right.

After all, this is going into the Design Document – as well as into the presentation I would prepare for the Project Steering Team's gate Review Meeting – and I want it to be the Voices of the Design Team that gets presented – and not some consultant's take on it.

I give the PST that too, but that's different.

Then I thank them – and send them all on their way – back to their day jobs!

After the Design Team Meeting

Post-design meeting activities involve:

- Documenting all meeting outputs
- Embellishing the "specs"
- Drafting the Modular Curriculum Development Design Document (see Chapter 15 for more information on this)
- Drafting the Project Steering Team Gate Review Meeting presentation
- Arranging for other, optional reviews of the Design Document

The Design Document describes the outputs of the design process and is presented and discussed at the Project Steering Team Phase 3 Gate Review Meeting.

The purpose of that meeting, attended by the Project Steering Team and perhaps one or more of the Design Team members or representatives of that team, is to review thoroughly the design details and then to approve, modify, or reject the design.

The document can be made available for expanded review and comment, such as by Design Review Teams.

When does a Project Manager or the PST want an expanded review? If only ten people out of a total audience of 3,000 global performers have been involved to this point, it may be politically wise to conduct more reviews.

These additional reviews bring feedback and create buy-in for the design prior to development/acquisition. Of course this should have been determined and planned for back in Phase 1.

The Analysis Team or other newly formed teams may be used as Design Review Teams to augment the work of the Project Steering Team.

A *series* of reviews may be held with *several* Design Review Teams. The design review process depends on the politics of the situation, existing Stakeholder groups, and their geographical dispersion.

Delivering the Design Document to reviewers prior to the review meeting is helpful, but most reviewers will not examine the document in detail prior to the meeting. It's sometimes preferable to "drag 'em through" the important and problematic details and design elements.

Depending on the length of the training being designed, it may not be feasible to review the entire design in detail. The facilitators must control the review process and keep the reviewers focused on the *key* elements of the design.

Managing reviewer expectations is critical. Reviewers must understand, for example, that the estimates of training times are "best guesses."

Reviewers must also understand that additional content may be factored into place as appropriate during development.

Does the Group Process for Design Work?

I've never had a design rejected, although sometimes it was close until Design Team members (handpicked by the Project Steering Team) took exception to the Project Steering Team taking exception to the work of the Design Team who was, after all, empowered.

Lesson Learned: **Trust the process!**

Hey, it's their design content, they *own the content*. We ISD'ers just *own the process* that got us to this point!

May the process be with you.

Chapter Summary & Transition

This chapter was intended to address the details of the Design phase of an MCD effort.

The outputs of the Design Phase are used to develop or acquire the T&D designed, for the purposes of Pilot-Testing.

The use of the Design Team meeting improves project cycle time; leads to higher quality, performance-based T&D through enhanced input from the Customer; and increases Customer ownership in the results of the project.

This chapter flows logically into the next, however your needs may cause you to want to skip around.

The following are the chapter titles and page numbers to assist you with your personal navigation needs.

Suggested Chapter Reflection & Reaction

I would suggest that prior to jumping into whichever chapter meets your needs that you give pause for a moment to reflect on the following and make some notes:

- Does this have applicability for me?

- What can I adopt from what I have read here?

- What are my potential needs for adaptation?

- What other issues do I see that I will need to address before embracing?

Please make note of your thoughts before proceeding.

Performance-based Modular Curriculum Development

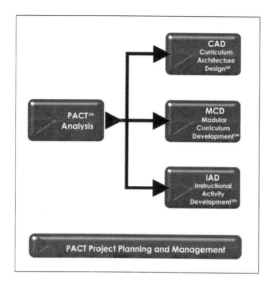

3 levels of ISD Methodologies
with common Analysis and
Project Planning & Management Methodologies.

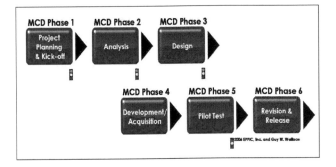

9 – PHASE 4: DEVELOPMENT

Chapter Overview

This chapter is intended to provide you with details regarding the Development phases of an MCD effort.

MCD Phase 4: Development/ Acquisition

The fourth phase of Modular Curriculum Development is Development/Acquisition.

Armed with a detailed set of Specs and Maps from which to build, and with detailed Performance Models and Knowledge/Skill Matrices for guidance, ISD developers work with a team of Master Performers and other Subject Matter Experts as needed to draft and refine the content of the instructional and informational materials for Pilot-Testing – unless that Phase is to be skipped or done stealthily.

Or, team members may use the documentation from Phase 3 to acquire - buy or reuse existing "as is" or "after modification" - training content and materials that fit the design specifications well enough as is, or close enough to modify.

Regardless of the deployment method chosen for the content, the designs are followed very closely as the instructional materials evolve.

Instructional materials developed during this phase might include Pilot-Test versions of:

- Participant/learner materials
- Instructor/facilitator materials
- Administrator materials
- Media masters
- Application exercise materials
- Evaluation materials
- Marketing materials

Miscellaneous ISD departmental reports may also be developed during this phase – depending on the others systems and processes unique to your Enterprise and T&D/L&D function.

Overview of MCD Phase 4: Development/ Acquisition

Description – In this phase, the training is developed, acquired, or modified according to the Design Document produced in Phase 3.

Key Activities/Tasks – Developers work with Subject Matter Experts and with any existing content to develop a pilot version of the training.

This phase should include "developmental testing" where warranted as determined by the developer or as is standard practice in their organization. That is the testing of the instructional components in isolation, versus the later Pilot-Test of the intact set of content – the entire Event.

Key Outputs – The outputs of this phase include all course materials appropriate to the media used, for example

- Participant Guides
- Facilitator Guides
- Administrator Guides
- Media masters
- Other materials depending on the media an modes
    - Videos
    - E-learning modules
    - Wall charts/posters
    - Exercise materials and formats
    - Etc.

Tasks for MCD Phase 4 – Development/Acquisition

The tasks of Phase 4 for Modular Curriculum Development are organized into four sub-phases.

Some changes to the tasks presented are inevitable, depending on the deployment platform for which the team is building. For example, at a micro-level, development activities for self-paced readings are different from development activities for an interactive e-learning program or webinar.

The framework of Phase 4, however, is appropriate to all media, modes of deployment, and deployment platforms.

MCD Subphase 4.1 – Predevelopment Planning, Data Gathering, and Preparation

This sub-phase ensures that anyone who is to be involved in development activities is fully up to speed on the design specs that will be used in developing the training.

In some projects, there is additional data gathering in this sub-phase, even though the data gathered and documented during the prior analysis and design efforts of a Curriculum Architecture Design might provide the Modular Curriculum Development effort *most* of the data and information needed.

But what if a whole new group of ISD developers is needed to get the project done by the targeted end date? The Performance Model is especially useful to bring the new developers up to speed on the terminal performance objectives for your project.

However, during T&D development, they will need to gather more micro-information from the assigned Subject Matter Experts and Master Performers on topics relevant to the particular T&D Modules assigned.

Most of the time, data gathering in the Development/Acquisition Phase of MCD is done using one-on-one or small-group interviews with Subject Matter Experts or Master Performers for specific tasks or Knowledge/Skill items.

The purposes of additional data gathering in this sub-phase are to

- Get specific "how-to" techniques for relevant situations.
- Find real-life examples to use in the training.
- Discover significant "variations" on the target task. For example, if the target task is to develop a budget, variations might include dealing with cross-department projects, currency exchange rates for international projects, a lack of available forecast data, ambiguity—whatever barriers to ideal performance exist.

MCD Subphase 4.2 – Development and Documentation

During this sub-phase, developers use the details of the Phase 3 design effort to build all of the piece-parts of the T&D Events and Lessons. Included in this effort is construction of the information content chunks, demonstrations, Performance Test and practice exercise activities, and written evaluation instruments.

One of the Phase 4 ground rules is that only *minor* changes to the Modular Curriculum Development design are allowed without asking for permission – and that being escalated as needed.

If developers and Subject Matter Experts are properly prepared in Subphase 4.1, and the developers are true ISD professionals, they should do just fine.

Subject Matter Experts and Master Performers from the Design Team can (hopefully) be restrained in their enthusiasm for massive redesign if they know that the Project Steering Team has sanctioned the design they're seeing.

The Project Manager's goal at this point of the Modular Curriculum Development process is to keep these changes *evolutionary* rather than *revolutionary*.

The Project Steering Team is told upfront that minor tweaking might occur after the design is approved based on what is uncovered during the microanalysis and micro-design efforts in the Development Phase.

MCD Subphase 4.3 – Developmental and Alpha Testing

During developmental and alpha testing, developers plan and conduct formal and informal testing of the piece-parts of the T&D. Not each T&D Lesson or Instructional Activity needs a formal developmental test—that would take too much time and too much money.

The Modular Curriculum Development Project Manager plans these appropriate tasks for certain elements of the design in this sub-phase – having left "room" in the schedule for such back in their Phase 1 planning efforts.

MCD Subphase 4.4 – Phase 4 Updates

During this sub-phase, the Development Team cleans up the T&D materials based on feedback from the formal and informal reviews held during developmental testing and alpha testing.

More Task Detail for Phase 4: Development/ Acquisition

Scan these detailed Task Listings for now – organized by the four sub-phases of Phase 4: Development, to simply become somewhat familiar with what's got to be done in this part of an MCD effort.

You will probably need to adapt this detailed listing – rather than adopt it for your context – when you are planning your first real project.

MCD Subphase 4.1 – Predevelopment Planning, Data Gathering, and Preparation

1. The Project Manager reviews the project with the assigned developers, providing all resource materials for their orientation and preparation.
2. The developers review the current Project Plan, the Analysis Report, the Design Document, and all other resource and background materials provided. The developers obtain additional materials and clarify (via phone or in person) as needed.

MCD Subphase 4.2 – Development and Documentation

1. Developers collect and review any and all existing T&D program materials to be reused or modified. These materials have been previously identified using T&D databases, paper files, libraries, T&D vendors, etc.

2. Developers coordinate logistics for any individual interviews needed for T&D content development. These interviews may be conducted with SMEs and MPs sanctioned by the Project Steering Team. The developers

    • Contact all interview participants and inform them of the project, purpose, outputs, process, and their specific roles.

    • Establish meeting methods, locations, dates, and times.

3. Developers prepare for and conduct individual interviews.

4. Developers develop initial T&D materials following the design framework. All materials are built consistent with the templates and go-by's provided by the ISD organization for the deployment platform designated. As appropriate to the platform, developers construct the following:

    • Participant materials
    • Instructor/facilitator materials
    • Administrator materials

5. The Project Manager updates plans as needed, then informs ISD management of any and all changes to the

    • Deployment Strategy and Plan
    • Evaluation Strategy and Plan

MCD Subphase 4.3 – Developmental and Alpha Testing

1. Development Team members (and others identified by the lead Subject Matter Expert/Master Performer or by the Project Steering Team) conduct formal and informal, in-progress developmental tests with SMEs/MPs.

2. Development Team members conduct formal and informal, in-progress developmental tests and reviews with the Project Manager, leads, and T&D organization management. The purpose of these tests and reviews is to assess the work of the development effort and identify any issues for the Project Steering Team to address. The Development Team assesses the appropriateness of and readiness for an alpha test.

3. The Project Manager coordinates logistics for the formal, pre-pilot test deployment alpha test with ISD management, key SMEs/MPs, and other Stakeholders. The Project Manager

   • Selects the alpha test location, dates, and times

   • Invites all participants and informs them about the project purpose, meeting purpose, outputs, process, and their specific roles

   • Confirms participant attendance immediately before the meeting date

   • Coordinates food, beverages, equipment, supplies, etc.

4. The Project Manager and perhaps the Development Team prepare for the conduct of the alpha test. This includes

   • Creating the alpha test kick-off presentation

   • Reviewing and critiquing the alpha test draft materials

     - Participant materials

     - Instructor/facilitator materials

- Administrative materials
- Reviewing and critiquing the
  - Deployment Strategy and Plans
  - Evaluation Strategy and Plans
- Summarizing changes to all materials

5.   The Development Team conducts the alpha test and checks all materials for

- Cultural fit
- Accuracy
- Completeness
- Effectiveness
- Readiness for the pilot-test deployment

MCD Subphase 4.4 – Phase 4 Updates

1.   In conjunction with ISD management and based on the feedback from the alpha test, the Project Manager determines all updates that are required to the materials developed.

2.   The Development Team updates all T&D materials according to feedback from the alpha test. As appropriate to the platform, the team may update the following:

- Participant materials
- Instructor/facilitator materials
- Administrator materials
- Deployment Strategy and Plan
- Evaluation Strategy and Plan
- Pilot-test Deployment and Evaluation Plan
- Pilot-test materials
  - Pilot-test brochure
  - Pilot-test evaluation materials

Alpha and Beta Testing/ Developmental Testing

Most products, training or not, are tested during development. The first round of formal testing is generally called alpha testing. The second round of organized testing on the more finished product is called beta testing. Beta testing is what ISD professionals sometimes call Pilot-Testing; but sometimes not.

I feel that training developers should perform internal and informal developmental or more formal tests during this phase as they see fit.

For example, it's usually worthwhile to try out exercises to insure that instructions are complete, that learners have enough information to answer typical procedural questions, that exercises are not too difficult or not too simple, and so forth.

However, some of the time the structure of the content— and the way it's expressed—is rather arbitrary; one approach will work just as well as another. Be aware that if you *ask* for opinions on content and expression during a developmental test, you will surely *get* those opinions, along with the consequent rework - and potential schedule slippage.

Unless you feel there are substantive issues on which you would like interim feedback, it may be better to let the Pilot Test in Phase 5 give you the feedback you want and need.

We suggest that for Phase 4 you subscribe to the realistic notion that you will deploy slight imperfection and then continuously improve, rather than deferring deployment for perfection.

That continuous improvement is what Phase 5 is all about.

No Low Value Walk-Throughs

I also have an opinion on whether to conduct those infamous, time-consuming, unnecessary walk-throughs of each and every page (or screen, etc.) of the training under development. These are a developer's nightmare.

A walk-through usually degenerates into "The Great Word-smithing Contest of Arbitrary Choices and Developer Disempowerment." In our experience, very few meaningful changes occur during a Phase 4 walk-through.

In fact, a walk-through usually increases cycle times, increases costs, detracts value, and demeans developers through the implied micromanagement of their work. Maybe in your situation they are needed, but I like to avoid them.

Instructional Activity Development Outputs

The outputs of an MCD Development phase are called: Instructional Activities. These include the following types of instructional activities, depending, of course, upon the project:

- Instructional content at the awareness, knowledge, or skill levels
- Demonstration of performance at the awareness, knowledge, or skill levels (these are in many ways "advanced organizers" prior to the Learners

applications
- Knowledge tests
- Performance tests
- Simulation exercises, case studies, games, etc.
- Performance aids
- Electronic or paper desk procedures

Each of these potential types of IAD outputs is described in more detail below.

Instructional Content at the Awareness, Knowledge, or Skill Levels

Most of the time, instructional content is developed within a Modular Curriculum Development project. The content may be at the awareness level, knowledge level, or skill level. However, in an Instructional Activity Development project, portions of instructional content can be developed separate from an entire training program.

What are the circumstances under which an Instructional Activity Development project might generate instructional content? Perhaps the T&D Customer needs to build content for immediate publishing, prior to releasing a more complete training package. Or maybe the entire T&D package is *just a maybe* . . . maybe it will be built and maybe it won't.

If it does end up being built, ISD'ers want the earlier content, demonstrations, or exercises to be compatible with the remainder of the course. The goal is to minimize additional downstream costs, yet to have the earlier content be *robust* to future add-ons.

Instructional content may be delivered at a non-training forum, such as a trade show or sales conference (for internal or external audiences), or at sales meetings, etc.

For the initial release of the training, some of the key content may be delivered at the next quarterly regional sales conference, with the related exercises occurring at a following conference.

This may not be ideal, but it may be the approach that has been chosen, and ISD will find itself complying with the Customers' wishes. It can be done using the Instructional Activity Development process if planned properly on the front end.

The Modular Curriculum Development lesson design methodology includes three types of instructional activities. Any of these are fair game for an Instructional Activity Development project.

- Information activities
- Demonstration activities
- Application activities

Activity Type	What It Provides	Examples
"Information Activity" within an MCD Lesson	A chunk of content/ information/facts, either in picture/diagram or in writing	• Instructional lectures • Instructional coaching • Self-paced readings • Video segments • Audio segments

Activity Type	What It Provides	Examples
"Demonstration Activity" within an MCD Lesson	An opportunity for the learner to see a *demonstration* of the performance, or some related aspect of it	• Live/verbal-*staged* presentations • Video-*staged* presentations • *Nonstaged* performance observations
"Application Activity" within an MCD Lesson	An *application* opportunity for the learner for practice and/or test purposes	• Games • Verbal quiz • Panel discussion/ dialogue • Paper and pencil tests • Case studies • Role-plays • Simulation exercises • Real work assignment

Lesson Map of Instructional Activities

The IA's - Instructional Activities' types and levels of depth can be seen/ assessed on a Lesson Map – see the example on the next page, repeated from earlier.

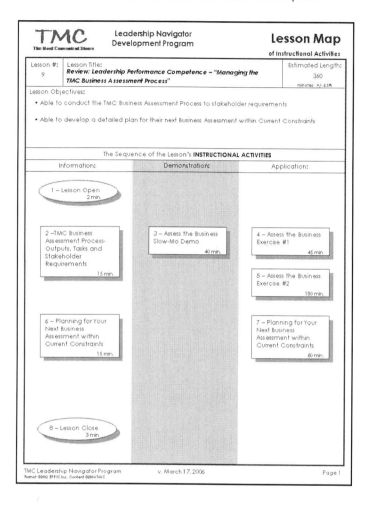

Knowledge Tests

The performance improvement need of the Customer may be quite narrow. Perhaps the Customer simply wants a series of performance-based, written knowledge tests to assess the knowledge base of incumbent populations in key job categories.

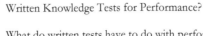

Written Knowledge Tests for Performance?

What do written tests have to do with performance-based T&D? Plenty. The knowledge measurable by written tests may be an enabler to key skills involved in performance. For example, calculating the amount of paint required to cover a room may be one of the things that enables a painter to pass a qualification test.

Knowledge tests are very familiar and vary in form, including:

- True/false
- Multiple choice
- Fill-in-the-blank
- Essay

The PACT Performance Model and Knowledge/Skill Matrix are the sources for formulating the right type of written test question.

The Performance Model indicates when a piece of knowledge is important for performance. So in the construction of written tests, developers are guided by the link between the knowledge item and its use in the performance situation.

The Performance Model and Knowledge/Skill Matrix assist in keeping the developer focused on performance first and content second. In turn, this helps ensure that the *test* is focused squarely on performance.

Performance Tests

Performance Tests measure individual performers' *real* capabilities and competency—or as near to real as it is feasible to get. They do this using testing instruments along with evaluation and assessment processes designed and developed to certify or qualify employees for certain types of performance.

These tests can include

- Performance demonstrations (real work)
- Performance simulations
- Talk-through troubleshooting

Performance Tests can deal with new real work, old real work, or simulations of real work.

Performance Demonstrations

Performance demonstrations are tests where learners demonstrate their ability to perform by actually doing something, usually with real work. This is the best test, of course, but it is not always feasible.

Performance Simulations

Real work is not always the best place to demonstrate competencies—emergency aircraft maneuvering, for example, or landing without the wheels down. Performance *simulations* allow testing of a learner's ability to perform under less than real conditions.

An example of a simulation is a classroom exercise involving negotiating with a supplier. The type of instructional activity called a simulation exercise, described later, can provide even more complexity (by design) than a performance simulation.

Talk-through Troubleshooting

In talk-through troubleshooting tests, learners *talk* their way through a series of diagnostic steps with an expert. This expert has a predetermined terminal condition in mind and answers the learner's troubleshooting questions accordingly.

For example, in response to an answer from a learner being tested on machinery operation, the expert may supply information such as: the valve gauge reads 10 and is slowly rising. The learner describes the next action to take and the expert provides feedback until the terminal condition is reached.

Like performance simulations, this type of test is useful when performing real work is not feasible. Performance Tests are developed more cheaply and quickly through this approach.

Other Methods for Performance Testing

In addition to the methods mentioned above, ISD professionals may use other methods for assessing performance capability. Among these are reviews of performance output, observations of the performer's processes, and debriefings of those involved in the performer's process—for example, debriefing the performer's Customer.

Other Uses for Performance Tests

A Performance Test can also be used as a component of an annual performance assessment process. A test instrument can be linked into many different performance management systems or perhaps to the appraisal systems already in place.

A Performance Test can also tighten up a loose process. A loose process is one in which performance variations exist but are undesirable. While some jobs can be evaluated solely on the basis of the product produced, most jobs are evaluated at least partly on the basis of how a product or output is produced, how much time or money is expended, or how procedures are followed. Performance Tests can help do that.

Sometimes Curriculum Architecture Design or Modular Curriculum Development projects begin as projects to construct Performance Tests for use as qualification or certification instruments.

Later, the scope of the project expands into a full CAD or MCD effort. Implementing performance-based testing can help T&D Customers see which specific areas of performance are good candidates for high-payback training developed using MCD.

Simulation Exercises

An Instructional Activity Development project may generate simulation exercises. Simulation exercises allow performers to simulate doing real work, although in a way that is broader and more complex than the performance simulation described earlier.

A simulation exercise might focus on a manager's role in the steps of progressive discipline. Managers who participate in this exercise may find themselves in a simulated series of individual interactions and meetings—sometimes alone with a union-represented individual, and other times with the individual and the local steward.

In other meetings, another management representative may take notes and act as a witness to the proceedings in case corroboration is needed later.

Learners may find themselves rotating through the various roles of a simulation exercise—for example, playing the union employee, the union steward, and so forth.

This allows participants to practice the target role and to gain insights from playing related roles. It also allows learners to observe and learn from the attempts by their fellow learners in the safety of an instructional event. A lot of "ah-ha's" happen in these types of simulation exercises.

Another type of simulation exercise might focus on the job of the project team leader for all of the phases of a product development process. Participants find themselves planning and conducting meetings in each of the process phases, dealing with typical issues (both problems and opportunities) that a team and leader face in a project.

As they rotate through the roles of engineering, manufacturing, sales, and service, participants gain functional insights from role-playing. They also have the opportunity to observe and learn as other participants attempt to lead their teams.

Simulation exercises test and build competency. They do this through an incremental Knowledge/Skills *build-up approach* to competency mastery that includes dealing with the real-world issues and barriers to high performance. It's often much better to practice in the relatively safe confines of T&D than to be experimenting with new behaviors and tasks on the job.

The components of a simulation exercise typically include the following, all of which are described below:

- Simulation exercise Datapaks
- Simulation exercise participant output formats and templates
- Simulation exercise facilitator tools and templates

Simulation Exercise Datapaks provide the learner with the simulation exercise instructions, examples of the outputs to be produced, background and scenario information, specific exercise data and information for use in the exercise, and a schedule for conducting the simulation exercise.

The simulation exercise *participant output formats and templates* are of the fill-in-the-blank nature that the exercise output may require. In general, the exercise instructions, process, and outputs should be tightly structured. The formats and templates help accomplish this.

Simulation exercise *facilitator tools and templates* can include observer critique sheets or checklists, answer guides, and even last-minute data additions of the "monkey-wrench" variety.

> "Your competitor has just brought out a product with these five features: . . ."

These monkey-wrench components are especially important if the real world often throws new obstacles (monkey wrenches) onto the path of superior performance and creates new, last-minute problems - and opportunities to flex and learn.

A simulation exercise can be used within a selection system as an in-basket exercise. This is literally a simulation of going through the items in an in-basket and attempting to deal with those items. As such, it is a test of the performer's capability to deal with the various realities of job performance.

Simulation exercises can be used as pretests or posttests within T&D. They can provide practice opportunities within T&D. And simulation exercises can give learners an opportunity to practice certain aspects of the job at varying levels of difficulty.

If the learning situation calls for the simulation of real work, the Instructional Activity Development process guarantees a focus on real performance.

Performance Aids/Job Aids

In some performance situations, the decision process is difficult due to the complexity of the question asked of the performer, the answer, or both. Sometimes the actual performance is not done very often.

These situations may require a performance aid to reduce cycle time and ensure the accuracy of the answer provided by the performer as one cannot expect them to commit it to memory for recall in the moment of need.

Performance-based performance aids (a.k.a. job aids or reference guides) can have a high return if they really work and are used as intended by the target audience.

Often the performance situation is an *open book* situation where performers have ready access to supplementary information. It may be that the performance aid is simply a formal version of the *cheat sheets* that many performers create for themselves (necessity being the mother of invention).

An Instructional Activity Development project may be conducted with the intent of producing no training but dozens or hundreds of performance aids.

Performance aids come in the following forms:

- Checklists
- Decision trees
- Process models and maps
- Tables or matrices
- Visual aids

Electronic or Paper Desk Procedures

A set of performance-based electronic desk procedures (just like performance aids or job aids) is often called an electronic performance support system (EPSS). These can have a high return if they work and are used by the target audience.

Electronic desk procedures are likely to be used in many different types of help desk or call center operations, where a quick response to complex, varied situations is needed, and where decision rules can be used to process a call correctly.

For example, when a credit card number is rejected in a sales situation, a call center operator might be able to quickly pull up the procedure for what to do next—e.g., resubmit the number, ask for another card number, or terminate the call.

Desk procedures may be on paper or accessed electronically. Mobile phones and computers make a great delivery platform for enabling the performers to access these as needed, in the moment of their need. Perhaps these needed prior instruction as to "how to use these" – perhaps not.

Let the Design Team make that call!

Chapter Summary & Transition

This chapter was intended to address the details of an MCD Development phase.

This chapter flows logically into the next, the Pilot Test Phase, however your needs may cause you to want to skip around.

The following are the chapter titles and page numbers to assist you with your personal navigation needs.

Suggested Chapter Reflection & Reaction

I would suggest that prior to jumping into whichever chapter meets your needs that you give pause for a moment to reflect on the following and make some notes:

- Does this have applicability for me?

- What can I adopt from what I have read here?

- What are my potential needs for adaptation?

- What other issues do I see that I will need to address before embracing?

Please make note of your thoughts before proceeding.

Guy W. Wallace

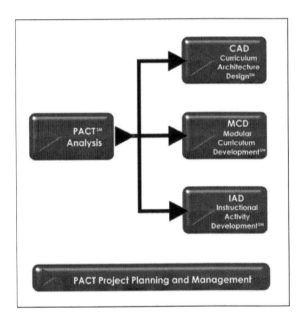

3 levels of ISD Methodologies
with common Analysis and
Project Planning & Management Methodologies.

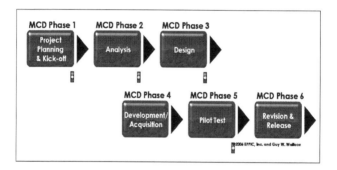

10 – PHASE 5: PILOT-TEST

Chapter Overview

This chapter is intended to provide you details about the MCD Pilot-Test phase.

MCD Phase 5: Pilot Test

Phase 5 of the Modular Curriculum Development effort is the Pilot Test. Depending on the mode of deployment, instructors, facilitators, and administrators prepare materials and themselves to conduct the Pilot Test.

As part of the preparation of the Learner, the overall learning experience is described to managers of pilot participants so that they in turn may do likewise. The managers are also informed of any post-pilot activities that must be completed to ensure successful transfer of Knowledge and Skills to the actual job, and their role and expectations are defined.

During the pilot-test session, written and verbal evaluations are collected and debriefings are conducted of the Learners, any facilitators, and any other key roles. After the session, the feedback is assessed and Revision Recommendations are generated for consideration by the Project Steering Team in their Gate Review Meeting.

The Project Steering Team may accept, modify, or reject the Revision Recommendations. The final results constitute the Revision Specifications used in the next and final phase of a Modular Curriculum Development project: Revision & Release.

Overview of MCD Phase 5: Pilot Test

Description – In Phase 5 of Modular Curriculum Development, the training is delivered during a pilot test, and extensive evaluations are conducted.

Key Activities/Tasks – Project activities in this phase include preparing for the pilot delivery (conducting train-the-trainer sessions, as appropriate); conducting the pilot test; evaluating the results of the pilot test; documenting the evaluations; and developing Revision Recommendations for the Project Steering Team. The Project Steering Team turns the recommendations into Revision Specifications.

Key Outputs – The outputs of this phase include

- The Pilot-Test Report
- A Project Steering Team presentation

Tasks for MCD Phase 5: Pilot Test

The tasks of Phase 5 for Modular Curriculum Development are organized into five sub-phases.

MCD Subphase 5.1 – Pre-pilot

In this sub-phase, the project team prepares for the pilot test. Preparations include coordinating logistics, producing materials, coordinating the personnel required for the pilot, setting up the pilot-test location, and doing final readiness checks.

MCD Subphase 5.2 – Pilot Deployment

During Subphase 5.2, pilot testing is conducted in circumstances that replicate how the T&D will be deployed once it's ready for general release to the marketplace.

Basically, the project team conducts the pilot test, coordinates the resolution of issues that arise, and conducts evaluations on the T&D being pilot-tested. Tasks in this sub-phase will vary depending on the chosen deployment platform (Mode, Media) and need to be adjusted accordingly by the Project Manager.

MCD Subphase 5.3 – Post-pilot Revision Recommendations

From this sub-phase comes a draft of the Revision Recommendations of the project's ISD professionals, based on a thorough review of the data collected during the pilot test. These Revision Recommendations are later reviewed and processed by the Project Steering Team.

MCD Subphase 5.4 – Pilot Phase Gate Review

In this sub-phase, the last formal meeting is held with the Project Steering Team for the Modular Curriculum Development effort. The Project Steering Team receives an overview of the phase along with the ISD Team's Revision Recommendations. The Project Steering Team's decisions and reactions to the recommendations evolve into a set of Revision Specifications for use in MCD's sixth phase, Revision & Release.

MCD Subphase 5.5 – Post-Gate Review

In this sub-phase, the Project Manager distributes the Revision Specifications and obtains sign-offs on the progress completed during the phase.

Now into the details.

More Task Detail for Phase 5: Pilot Test

Scan these detailed Task Listings for now – organized by the four sub-phases of Phase 5: Pilot-Test, to simply become somewhat familiar with what's got to be done in this part of an MCD effort.

You will probably need to adapt this detailed listing – rather than adopt it for your context – when you are planning your first real project.

MCD Subphase 5.1 – Pre-pilot

1. The Project Manager coordinates logistics for the pilot-test deployment, based on the deployment platform. The Project Manager

   • Selects the pilot-test deployment method, locations, dates, and times

   • Invites all participants and orients them to the project purpose, the pilot-test deployment purpose, outputs, process, and their specific roles

   • Confirms pilot-test participant attendance immediately before the pilot-test deployment date

   • Coordinates food, beverages, equipment, supplies, etc.

2. The Project Manager initiates production of the materials necessary to conduct the initial pilot-test deployment (consistent with the deployment platform) using ISD departmental standards.

3. The Project Manager coordinates the personnel requirements for the pilot-test deployment. While these requirements may vary depending on the deployment platform, the deployment strategy, and the tactical plan, the Project Manager must generally schedule, orient, and develop personnel for the roles of

   • Instructor and/or facilitator

   • Administrator

4. Instructors and facilitators prepare for their roles. To do this, they

- Collect all materials required for delivery or facilitation.
- Review the Instructor/Facilitator's Guide and other materials.
- Obtain basic platform skills (as needed).
- Conduct practice dry runs (as needed).
5. The administrator prepares for his or her role. The administrator
    - Collects all materials required for the administration of the pilot-test deployment
    - Reviews the Administrator's Guide and other relevant materials
6. The Project Manager coordinates the preparation and setup for the pilot-test deployment. The Project Manager
    - Prepares sites (rooms, labs, desktops, workplaces, homes, etc.) appropriate for the deployment platforms
        - Seating/tables requirements
        - Equipment
        - Materials
        - Etc.
    - Conducts a check of the readiness of instructors and facilitators
    - Confirms pilot-test participant attendance
    - Invites backup participants as needed, confirming their attendance
7. The Project Manager confirms attendance of all participants, and coordinates arrangements for any replacement participants using the backup candidate list.

MCD Subphase 5.2 – Pilot Deployment

1. The Development Team conducts the pilot test according to the previously developed plan.
2. The Development Team coordinates the resolution of any pilot-test issues that may arise.
3. The pilot team conducts all evaluations (verbal debriefs, written evaluations, etc.) according to the pilot-test evaluation plan.

MCD Subphase 5.3 – Post-pilot Revision Recommendations

1. The Project Manager and/or the ISD Team conduct a post-pilot-test deployment review of all evaluation data. The data includes

   • Written evaluation from pilot-test participants

   • Written evaluation from instructors and facilitators

   • Daily verbal feedback

2. The Project Manager drafts Revision Recommendations for review with ISD management, as needed. The Project Manager drafts the Pilot-Test Report using the PACT Process go-by's and templates. If appropriate, a preliminary version of the report is distributed for review and comment prior to the Gate Review Meeting held in the next sub-phase.

MCD Subphase 5.4 – Pilot Phase Gate Review

1. The Project Manager coordinates logistics for the Project Steering Team Phase 5 Gate Review Meeting, including

   • Meeting method, location, dates, and times

   • Arrangements for meeting materials, equipment, and food and beverage

- Invitations and communications about
  - Date, time, location, and directions
  - Accommodations for travel, living, meals, etc.
  - The project, meeting purpose, outputs, process, specific roles, and any preparations required on the part of meeting participants
2. The Project Manager confirms participant attendance immediately before the meeting date.
3. The Project Manager prepares to conduct the Project Steering Team Phase 5 Gate Review Meeting. Preparations include
- Agendas
- Gate review presentation materials and all handout materials
- Assignments
- Briefings
4. The Project Manager conducts the Project Steering Team Phase 5 Gate Review Meeting. In doing this, he or she
- Reviews the project purpose, business drivers, approach, process, deliverables, and schedule for key milestones
- Reviews all actuals compared to plan, provides a rationale for all deviations, and discusses the implications of the project's cost and schedule performance
- Reviews
  - The pilot-test process specifics and participants
  - Evaluation summaries and specifics
  - Revision recommendations from the project ISD Team
- Obtains the Project Steering Team's input concerning the ISD Team's Revision Recommendations, and based on that input creates the Revision Specifications

- Identifies all other key project issues (problems, opportunities, goals, constraints, etc.)
- Reviews any and all change recommendations, and their rationale, for the Deployment Strategy and Plan
- Assesses the phase completion status using the Phase 5 exit criteria

5.   The Project Manager documents the Revision Specifications from the Project Steering Team.

MCD Subphase 5.5 – Post-Gate Review

1.   The Project Manager updates the Pilot-Test Report based on the feedback from the Project Steering Team leadership, including the Revision Specifications. The Project Manager forwards the report to all members of the Project Steering Team, to ISD management, and to other Stakeholders, including the developers and Development Team members affected by the Revision Specifications.

2.   The Project Manager obtains sign-offs from ISD management and from the Customer, the Project Steering Team chairperson.

Pilot-Test Debriefings & Evaluations

You will need to conduct debriefings and evaluations of the Pilot-Tests using minimally your standard evaluation methods and tools. You probably need to conduct much more evaluation than you normally do.

I generally include both written and verbal evaluations/debriefings in my methods; but always defer to what my Clients use – unless they see mine as more appropriate for their needs.

I do "written evaluations" for each lesson be that face-to-face or online. I do end of day/session written evaluations and then verbal debriefings.

The goal is always to generate Pilot-Test Results data that you can use to formulate the Revision Recommendations for the Project Steering Team to consider – for their approval or modification.

There have been a few times when my recommendation to the PST was to ignore some of the feedback from the Pilot-Test participants – and I had to make a business case for that recommendation to ignore the Voice of the Learners. I showed them the data.

One time I explained why I thought we should ignore the feedback – despite it being very clear. That feedback I explained was simply part of an overall resistance early in the instruction that was more related to their dislike in the change that the "instruction" was related to.

Participants wanted to skip some of the early hands-on exercises and wanted them out – but only because they didn't want to see their familiar system being replaced for a "pilot-testing" of a new system. The data pattern changed later in the session, a bit. But overall they didn't want hands-on exercises. They wanted to sit and listen and be done with it as soon as possible.

It's a business decision to ignore the data at times.

Chapter Summary & Transition

This chapter was intended to address the details of the Pilot-Test phase of an MCD effort.

This chapter flows logically into the next, however your needs may cause you to want to skip around.

The following are the chapter titles and page numbers to assist you with your personal navigation needs.

Suggested Chapter Reflection & Reaction

I would suggest that prior to jumping into whichever chapter meets your needs that you give pause for a moment to reflect on the following and make some notes:

- Does this have applicability for me?

- What can I adopt from what I have read here?

- What are my potential needs for adaptation?

- What other issues do I see that I will need to address before embracing?

Please make note of your thoughts before proceeding.

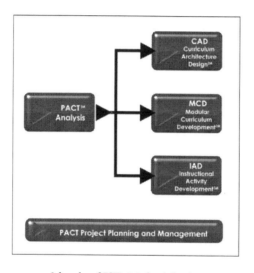

3 levels of ISD Methodologies
with common Analysis and
Project Planning & Management Methodologies.

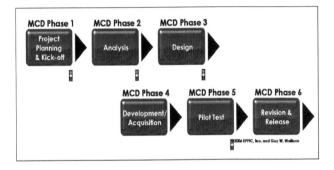

11 – PHASE 6: REVISION & RELEASE

Chapter Overview

This chapter is intended to provide you the details for conducting the final phase of an MCD effort.

Overview of Phase 6: Revision & Release

Description – In this phase, all materials are updated according to the Revision Specifications from Phase 5. The materials are then released into that segment of the training system that manages deployment.

Key Activities/Tasks – Activities in this phase include updating the training materials and releasing the materials to all areas of training, e.g., registration information, material masters, etc.

Key Outputs – The outputs of this sub-phase include the training material masters for

- Participant Guides
- Facilitator Guides
- Administrator Guides
- Media masters
- Other materials
    - E-learning content
    - Coaches/ Mentors Packages
    - Webinar masters and scripts
    - Wall charts/Posters
    - Exercise instructions, reading materials, output templates/ formats
    - Etc.

MCD Phase 6: Revision & Release

The sixth phase of a Modular Curriculum Development project is Revision & Release.

The Revision Specifications approved by the Project Steering Team in Phase 5 determine the final updates required of all of the materials.

After revision, master materials are stored for duplication, assembly, and deployment.

Tasks for MCD Phase 6 – Revision & Release

The tasks of Phase 6 for Modular Curriculum Development are organized into four sub-phases.

MCD Subphase 6.1 – Materials Revision

During Subphase 6.1, the Development Team updates the T&D materials, following the Revision Specifications. Then paper and electronic "masters" are produced for the T&D materials.

MCD Subphase 6.2 – Materials Release

In this sub-phase, all T&D materials are delivered to the organizations that will deploy the T&D.

MCD Subphase 6.3 – Lessons Learned Documentation and Distribution

In this sub-phase, project management conducts an analysis of lessons learned from the Modular Curriculum Development project just completed. These lessons learned are documented and distributed.

MCD Subphase 6.4 – Project Data Compilation and Archiving

This sub-phase involves cleanup, where project data is gathered and archived, either electronically or as paper.

More Task Detail for Phase 6: Revision & Release

Scan these detailed Task Listings for now – organized by the four sub-phases of Phase 6: Revision & Release, to simply become somewhat familiar with what's got to be done in this part of an MCD effort.

You will probably need to adapt this detailed listing – rather than adopt it for your context – when you are planning your first real project.

MCD Subphase 6.1 – Materials Revision

1. The Development Team updates all materials following the Revision Specifications from the Phase 5 Project Steering Team Gate Review Meeting. The team updates, as appropriate to the platform, the following:

   • Participant materials
   • Instructor/facilitator materials
   • Administrator materials
   • Deployment Strategy and Plans
   • Evaluation Strategy and Plans

2. The Development Team produces paper masters and electronic files for all materials. These are transferred to the ISD organization for ongoing delivery, administration, and continuous improvement through content updating.

MCD Subphase 6.2 – Materials Release

1. The ISD development organization then forwards all materials to the organization responsible for administering delivery and access of the T&D.
2. The organization responsible for administering delivery and access forwards all materials to the appropriate delivery/deployment organization according to the current Deployment Strategy and Plan.

MCD Subphase 6.3 – Lessons Learned Documentation and Distribution

1. The Project Manager conducts a post-project analysis of lessons learned using meetings, surveys, and other appropriate methods. All key project participants and Stakeholders are involved, including

  • Customers and Stakeholders

  • ISD organization staff

  • Others as appropriate

2. The Project Manager documents all lessons learned and forwards the documentation to ISD management.
3. ISD management distributes the lessons learned as appropriate.

MCD Subphase 6.4 – Project Data Compilation and Archiving

1. The Project Manager gathers all project data, archiving it or entering it into databases (paper and electronic) following ISD organization standards and guidelines.
2. The Project Manager informs those with a need to know about the project completion, data gathered during the project, and file storage.

Chapter Summary & Transition

This chapter was intended to address the details for Phase 6 of an MCD effort.

This chapter flows logically into the next, about the infrastructure and environmental supports needed to conduct ISD via the MCD processes, however your needs may cause you to want to skip around.

The following are the chapter titles and page numbers to assist you with your personal navigation needs.

Suggested Chapter Reflection & Reaction

I would suggest that prior to jumping into whichever chapter meets your needs that you give pause for a moment to reflect on the following and make some notes:

- Does this have applicability for me?

- What can I adopt from what I have read here?

- What are my potential needs for adaptation?

- What other issues do I see that I will need to address before embracing?

Please make note of your thoughts before proceeding.

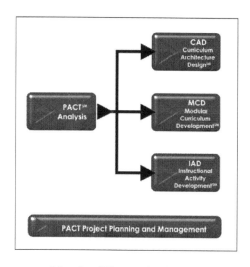

3 levels of ISD Methodologies
with common Analysis and
Project Planning & Management Methodologies.

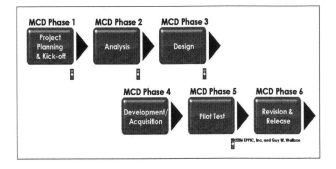

12 – MCD INFRASTRUCTURE AND ENVIRONMENTAL SUPPORT REQUIREMENTS

Chapter Overview

This chapter is intended to provide you an overview of the infrastructure and environmental supports necessary for success in MCD efforts.

In this chapter we will cover the following:

- The 5-Tier Inventory Framework
- The WELL
- Lesson & Instructional Activity Number Scheme
- Titling Schemes

5-Tier Inventory Framework

This one set of "data drawers" from an Enterprise Content Architecture database.

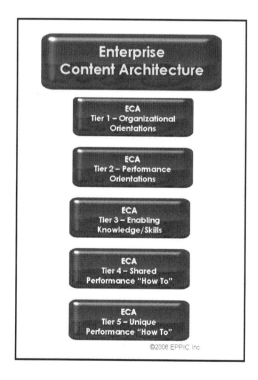

The 5 Tier Inventory Scheme/ Framework is an organizing scheme for keeping the piece parts of an Intact Event in an inventory scheme (framework) that makes it easier for Analysts, Designers and Developers find content for their assessments for Reuse purposes – where they decide either to reuse "as is" (AI) or "after modification" (AM – or "not at all" (NA). An event is really one or more Lessons which are themselves a set of Instructional Activities. The 5 Tier Inventory Framework is a Data Logic scheme for tracking these..

Tier 1 mirrors the Enterprise's organizational structure – from The Enterprise, and Business Units/Divisions, Functions, Departments, Jobs and Teams.

As it – those organizational entities – change, the boundary conditions and content of these Instructional Activities (IAs) change in parallel. There are no derivatives. But there is a great deal of patterning – per like levels in this hierarchy. All Functional Overviews should have the same template with the same level of detail – for a common look and feel although the content is about unique organizations.

Tier 2 and 4 and 5 content require real performance analysis to be conducted.

Tier 2 items match the combination of all 4s and 5s.

Tier 2s provide the "advanced organizers" before someone learns Tier 3's on the way to then learning the integration and application of all to the Performance that is shared or unique in a Tier 4 or 5.

The Tier 2 content, "Performance Orientations" are easily well designed – based on the analysis data from Phase 2. It establishes the Performance Objectives of Performance Competence, and ties all of the other learning objects/modules at the front end of the "instructional" – as an advanced organizer.

Tier 4 and 5 content are the real "How To" – and the only differences is the number of audiences one has versus the other.

Tier 3 houses all of the enabling K/Ss. In my 30+ years in the business – this is where almost all Enterprise Learning resources have been invested, as evidenced by my Analysis Phases' ETA efforts – that Existing T&D Assessment effort.

And rather than lead to Tier 4 and 5 content – they are taught/delivered in a generic fashion – with less authenticity than the "authentic enough" needed to help ensure transfer. These items are not designed themselves in a modular fashion to enable plug-n-play swapping of the definitions, examples, demonstrations and applications exercises to make them authentic enough – and thus lead to lots of redundancy.

Here there should be many derivatives (by design) rather than overlapped and gapped redundancy, inadvertently, but a waste of shareholder equity none-the-less.

Not good stewardship.

Once a client had 26 two hour Modules on Active Listening. Not tailored to any one particular job. Just 26 versions of the same thing with very slight differences.

A well designed Enterprise Content (Instruction and Information) Architecture and T&D Paths is more than just a collection of courses, modular or not.

And it is more than a collection of Modules.

Managing all of the piece parts of instruction and information – requires a way to administrate, track, original content, and potentially many derivatives of that original content.

If your system isn't designed to manage – and encourage – derivatives – then you will forgo maximizing authenticity and performance impact – and your content similarity won't be truly an enabler of reuse. You'll end up with a lot of inadvertent redundancy.

And that's not good stewardship.

The WELL

The WELL is my name for where I keep all of the **Masters** and **derivatives** for all photos, graphics, standard text, etc.

They are reusable too – and they are objects – but I draw the line at formally designing reuse at the Instructional Activity level even though in reality it happens at a couple of lower levels.

Think: a photo of the current CEO plus text on her biography, plus a graphic that she likes to show in every presentation she has ever made since getting to the top – and will likely continue to use.

You don't want to reinvent any of these over and over again – and you don't want to do endless searches only to inadvertently find and use a derivative (the wrong thing) versus the original that you wanted – or you find the wrong derivative when there was "that one derivative" that you know is perfect for your needs!

These WELL items are also "objects" in an object oriented design. They are just "below the water line" in the PACT Processes approach to object oriented design. Plus the WELL stores all of the templates, such as Performance Models and Enabling K/S Matrices, etc.

Think: go to the well for fresh water/resources. Or the stored derivatives – and hasten your efforts – and don't waste your time in long searches or reinventing any wheels/ objects.

I've been using the WELL concept since the mid-1980s – after being exposed to one client's Coming to Terms binder

– where the standard Contracts and already approved, by Legal, derivatives were made available for their sales force.

> Can you imagine the cycle time reductions that this Sales Force had with these pre-approved derivatives for Contract language allowing them to "avoid the lawyers like the plague!"

That's where the credit goes for my concept of The WELL.

Lesson & Instructional Activity Numbering Scheme

You need to create a numbering scheme that allows you to track and find and store Content items – more quickly and effectively.

The Tier numbers help start that scheme – but the anticipated volume of Content and the number of Target Audiences make this a challenge for many.

Tier 1- numbering needs to reflect the Organization structure. Think: Organization chart.

Tier 2- numbering needs to reflect the Target Audiences. Think: HR's job family numbering scheme.

Tier 3- numbering needs to reflect the K/S Categories after any adaptations required. See the graphic below – from my book on The PACT Process for Performance-based Curriculum Architecture Design.

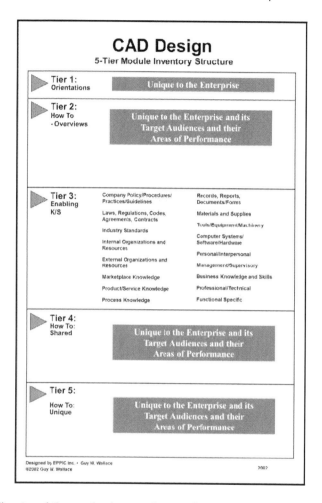

Tier 4 and 5- numbering needs to reflect the Target Audiences. Think: HR's job family numbering scheme.

These Tier 4 and 5 items need to match exactly the Tier 2 numbering scheme: for every Tier 2 item there is either a Tier 4 or a Tier 5 item.

After that start with the Tier number, I would have a code that targeted deeper levels of a category scheme, and take into account potential derivative's.

The coding can be as complex as needed – and simplified by using understood patterns.

Titling Schemes for Instructional Activities, Lessons, Modules and Events

Truth in titling is a motto of the PACT Processes. That lets the buyer (Learner) beware - and be informed.

All Content in PACT is at three levels of depth:

1.   Awareness
2.   Knowledge
3.   Skill.

Events, Modules/Lessons and Instructional Activities are either named with a **preface phrase** - or not.

That **preface phrase** is either:

- Overview of:
- How to:

Overview of: means this is an **Awareness level** of content. In other words, this might not be enough for your needs.

> For example, perhaps the VP of L&D needs: Overview of: Managing the TMC New Product Development Process.

How to: signifies that this is at a **Skill level** of content. In other words, you might need less.

For example, perhaps the new Engineering Manager needs: How To: Managing the TMC New Product Development Process.

If there **no preface phrase** that means that it is at the **Knowledge level** of depth.

For example, perhaps the Instructional Analyst needs: The TMC New Product Development Process.

Think about scanning a T&D Path for your first acid test – the sniff test – would this type of labeling help you decide whether you liked it, what you saw in that first pass, or not?

I don't like cutesy titles – and there are way too many of them in my business. Save those cute titles for the sub-titles. Let the main title tell it like it is.

Chapter Summary & Transition

This chapter was intended to address the infrastructure and environmental support needed to facilitate/enable CAD efforts. We covered:

- The 5-Tier Inventory Framework
- Module Number Scheme
- Titling Schemes

You might need to adapt what was presented here rather than merely adopt what was presented.

This chapter flows logically into the next on ISD Supplier Teams and their Roles, however your needs may cause you to want to skip around.

The following are the chapter titles and page numbers to assist you with your personal navigation needs.

Suggested Chapter Reflection & Reaction

I would suggest that prior to jumping into whichever chapter meets your needs that you give pause for a moment to reflect on the following and make some notes:

- Does this have applicability for me?

- What can I adopt from what I have read here?

- What are my potential needs for adaptation?

- What other issues do I see that I will need to address before embracing?

Please make note of your thoughts before proceeding.

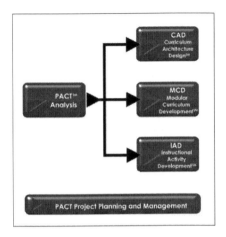

3 levels of ISD Methodologies
with common Analysis and
Project Planning & Management Methodologies.

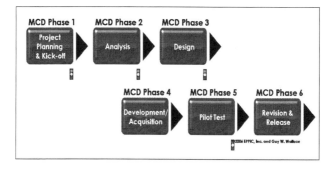

13 – MCD SUPPLIER TEAMS AND ROLES

Chapter Overview

This chapter is intended to provide you with a definition of the key roles and responsibilities of the ISD Supplier staff in conducting MCD efforts.

The PACT Processes are accelerated partially due to their use of teams with predefined roles and responsibilities. Individuals and teams with agreed-to accountabilities are a critical element in the planning and management of the PACT Processes for T&D.

While a successful T&D development project is dependent on the quality of the Project Plan, it is critical to have the right people to do the right things at the right time, according to plan.

The Use of Teams

The PACT Processes' structure spells out the teams and roles necessary to ensure the right people handle everything at the right time in the process.

There are teams for ISD Customers and one team for the ISD Suppliers – one team with four key roles.

Those teams and roles for the ISD Customers are covered in the next chapter. Here we will focus on the ISD Supplier Team and their key Roles.

Roles versus Jobs

A role is not a job. One individual can play one or more of the roles defined in any particular project.

There have been many projects where I have acted in all of the ISD roles mentioned in this chapter; many projects where each role was played by a different person; and some projects where for some roles there were many individuals working in that role, e.g., many developers.

The ISD Team

The ISD team works with members of other teams during all phases of PACT Processes projects. The ISD Team is staffed by ISD practitioners (or instructional technologists).

ISD team members plan and manage the project, as well as conduct the meetings and pilot-test sessions. They do the ISD work, own the ISD processes being used, and work with the Customers and Stakeholders who own the content of the T&D to be produced.

Members of the ISD Team provide a mixed knowledge and skill set that is very powerful. When not combined appropriately, however, much can be lost at a great expense of time and money.

The MCD Project Manager Role

Besides the Project Steering Team chairperson, another role on the team is the Project Manager. The role of the Project Manager is to manage the interaction between the Customer organization and ISD professionals. For example, the Project Manager helps an Analyst get in touch with the right people to find out about the nature of the jobs targeted for study. In addition, the Project Manager contacts all team members to inform them of their participation and roles in the project.

It's up to the Project Manager to plan well, communicate the plan, and *sell* the plan. This keeps everyone on the same wavelength, with common goals and expectations.

The specific responsibilities of the Project Manager include activities such as

- Gathering all internal information as identified during the conduct of the project
- Coordinating the logistics for all interviews and meetings; for example, location and space arrangements

One person may fill the role of Project Manager. However, in certain projects, it makes sense to have two individuals in this role, one from the Customer organization and one from the supplier (ISD) organization.

The First Project Steering Team Meeting

Project Steering Team members may be recruited by the Project Manager or, in the ideal case, by the Project Steering Team chairperson. The chairperson's credibility and organizational responsibility can be a big advantage in recruiting.

If the Project Manager recruits potential members, he or she should make arrangements for the first meeting of the Project Steering Team before making recruiting calls. In contacting prospective members, the Project Manager should know the potential location of the first meeting (and have at least two alternative dates to propose) and know the meeting length (no more than two hours for this first meeting). The Project Manager should make detailed copies of the Project Plan available in advance.

At the first meeting, the Project Manager should be prepared to present the Project Plan in summary fashion and must *sell* Project Steering Team members on the project. The task is to demonstrate an understanding of

- The performance situation the project is to address
- The implications of the current situation

- The magnitude of the implications
- The payoff for resolving the situation

The most critical information here is the payoff, the returns on the investment for resolving the situation.

It's up to the Project Manager to anticipate Project Steering Team member views, identify the pros and cons of alternative approaches, rank the alternatives, and be prepared to answer tough questions with logic, poise, and determination. Once the Project Steering Team is on board, gaining commitment and cooperation from other project participants is much easier.

At the first and subsequent Project Steering Team meeting, it's good technique for the Project Manager to engage in constructive confrontation. By forewarning the team of his or her intentions, the Project Manager gets the attention of the team and receives its feedback on those intentions.

The MCD Analyst Role

The Analyst role is central to generating good data from the Analysis Team. The ISD professional in this role leads and facilitates the structured, analytic methods in the Analysis Team meeting and conducts some of the analyses outside the Analysis Team meeting. The data gathered by the Analyst is used to generate an Analysis Report.

The selection, training, and assessment of the individuals for this role is of supreme concern to the Project Manager. Group facilitation skills are critical! In some cases, the Project Manager may be the Analyst.

The MCD/IAD Designer Role

The MCD/IAD Designer role is similar to the CAD Designer role, except that it is in this capacity that the ISD practitioner practices what is closest to the traditional ISD design job—designing T&D! Again, facilitation skills, communication capabilities, and lack of ego are key issues for the selection of Designers for this role.

Often, the same individual may fill the Analyst and Designer roles. However, a good Analyst may make a lousy Designer and vice versa. The skill sets overlap, but there are some key differences.

The MCD/IAD Lead Developer Role

The MCD/IAD Lead Developer role within PACT is very traditional.

The biggest difference is that the developer and the Development Team that they lead have a very detailed design spec and map to follow when they build the materials.

They can't waver from the design arbitrarily, because the entire content configuration may be sub-optimized.

They can spend their creative energies not on segmenting content and arranging flow, but on sound instructional design for the lessons assigned to them—lessons that include informational segments, demonstration segments, and application segments.

The Pilot-Test Team Member Roles

The purpose of the Pilot-Test Team is to conduct a pilot test following the initial development of the T&D. The Pilot-Test Deployment Team includes instructors, facilitators, and administrators who conduct the pilot session. The Pilot-Test Deployment Team is used in Modular Curriculum Development and Instructional Activity Development.

Pilot-Test Deployment Team members coordinate all logistics for facilities, equipment, media, food and beverages, invitations, and confirmations for the attendees. They also deliver the instruction or oversee the instructional delivery for the purposes of pilot testing. (Pilot-Test Deployment Team members cannot, in general, make changes during delivery *on the fly*.) Finally, they conduct written and verbal evaluations and debriefings to gather feedback for revision purposes.

There are two types of pilot-test facilitators and instructors.

- Lead pilot-test facilitators and instructors
- Guest pilot-test facilitators and instructors

Lead facilitators are assigned specific lessons for delivery administration, depending on the deployment method of the design. Lead facilitators typically come from the ranks of the project's Subject Matter Experts.

Guest facilitators are brought in to teach specialized subjects in specific modules or lessons. For example, in a course on product management, a representative of the corporate finance department may teach a lesson on measuring return on investment. Guest facilitators may or may not be lead or review Subject Matter Experts.

Chapter Summary & Transition

This short chapter was intended to address the ISD Customer Roles in an MCD effort.

This chapter flows logically into the next, however your needs may cause you to want to skip around.

The following are the chapter titles and page numbers to assist you with your personal navigation needs.

Suggested Chapter Reflection & Reaction

I would suggest that prior to jumping into whichever chapter meets your needs that you give pause for a moment to reflect on the following and make some notes:

- Does this have applicability for me?

- What can I adopt from what I have read here?

- What are my potential needs for adaptation?

- What other issues do I see that I will need to address before embracing?

Please make note of your thoughts before proceeding.

Guy W. Wallace

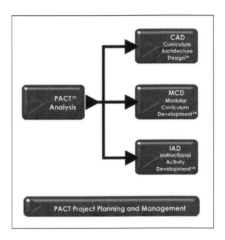

3 levels of ISD Methodologies
with common Analysis and
Project Planning & Management Methodologies.

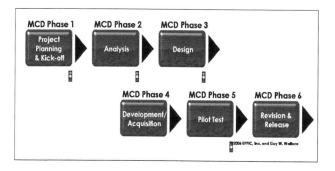

14 – MCD CUSTOMER TEAMS AND ROLES

Chapter Overview

This chapter is intended to provide you with an overview of the key ISD Customer Teams and key Roles for an MCD effort.

These Teams and Roles that we are going to cover include:

- Project Steering Team
- Project Steering Team Chairperson
- Project Steering Team Members
- Analysis Team
- Analysis Review Team
- Design Team
- Design Review Team
- Pilot Test Team

The Project Steering Team

Arguably the most important team in any PACT project is the **Project Steering Team**, composed of Customers and other key Stakeholders.

The most critical step of Phase 1 within any one of the PACT Processes is recruiting, organizing, and communicating with the Project Steering Team.

The successful selection and organization of Project Steering Team members leads to the ability to communicate collectively with them regarding the project.

Project Steering Team members, in turn, carefully consider and then select all of the other individuals for staffing the rest of the project's roles.

The Project Steering Team

The Project Steering Team is typically responsible for

- "Owning" the project
- Reviewing the Project Plan and directing the project

- Selecting all participants for later phases of the project
- Reviewing and providing feedback for all project documents and outputs

The Project Manager uses the Project Steering Team to test ideas and obtain sanctioning for all project activities via the Gate Review Meetings.

The members of the Project Steering Team review, debate, and challenge as necessary the MCD Project Plan. Team members also assist in making available the human resources data and other data needed to conduct the project. In addition, they select all of the other PACT team members.

Project Steering Team roles and responsibilities are similar in Curriculum Architecture Design, Modular Curriculum Development, and Instructional Activity Development. In each case, the team is composed of members who have a stake in the outcomes and process for conducting the PACT Process project. And in each case, the most important role on the Project Steering Team is that of chairperson.

The Project Steering Team Chairperson

In general, the Project Steering Team chairperson is the logical owner of the project, the person with responsibility and accountability for making change happen. This person will possibly be evaluated by his or her management based on the success of the project.

Organizational etiquette suggests that the PACT Project Manager, the planner of the process leading to that success or failure, must understand how score is kept for the Client.

The Project Steering Team chairperson is the key Customer/Stakeholder interface and helps identify all other key Stakeholders that should be involved in the project. Early in the project, this person provides key input for the development of the Project Plan.

The Project Steering Team chairperson also helps identify other individuals that he or she thinks may be necessary to involve in the conduct of the project. They, too, should be engaged up-front. Many of these key Stakeholders may be the future members of the Project Steering Team.

Project Steering Team Members

Project Steering Team members nominally include key leaders of the organizations within the scope of the project. To accomplish its tasks, the Project Steering Team must be composed of the highest level individuals who may benefit from or be affected by the project.

The goal is not to get the company CEO on the project, but to get other people with the right authority levels and interest— those with authority to prioritize and then provide dollars and people for the follow-on T&D projects. But in addition to authority, the Project Manager wants the *participation* of Stakeholders.

The Project Manager wants those with *something at stake* in the outcomes of the T&D project; those who will have to live with the consequences of doing nothing, doing the wrong thing, or doing the right thing. Those with something at stake could include Customers of a process; suppliers; and support organizations such as information systems, field operations, human resources, etc.

In selecting candidates for the Project Steering Team, the general rule is to determine who might come forward sometime during the project and question or take exception to what is happening. Better to invite them on day one to have their say and attempt to influence the Project Steering Team. Having them join the fray two months into the project is never ideal.

If a project hits close to their home, candidates who are true Stakeholders might be so intrigued by the thought and structure of the planned effort that they might be willing to participate—*if* they see a return for their investment. Maybe they'll need to delegate participation. But the goal is to bring in representatives of all key groups!

How many members are on a Project Steering Team? The fewer members, the faster things may move. The more members, the less likelihood any one individual can negatively influence the project. It's a balancing act.

Establishing a formal Project Steering Team ensures that key Stakeholders "buy in" to the Project Plan politically, that it makes business sense, and that the outputs and planned tasks will be supported during and after the project. The Project Steering Team handpicks all other team members, and that goes a long way to ensuring that the outputs produced by those teams have credibility. That is extremely important because the volume of data in the outputs produced makes it problematic that the Project Steering Team will be able to do a thorough review. Besides, it's better to build in quality early than to attempt to inspect it in later.

The Project Steering Team and "Command and Control"

PACT projects are structured so that participants are empowered—within certain boundaries and limits. The Project Steering Team provides many of those boundaries and limits. By their actions, Project Steering Team members help to provide "command and control" for the PACT project.

Command and control is an old, and some would say outdated, paradigm. But even with empowerment and flat organizational structures, it's necessary to have a way to provide clear direction, to gather strategic input from leaders and Stakeholders, and to resolve conflicts among Stakeholders. Without command and control, the project ship would drift aimlessly, never reaching its destination.

The Project Steering Team and its gate reviews embody command and control. They allow the voice of the Customer from the upper levels of the organization to be taken into account.

They allow for the discovery and resolution of conflict among T&D Customers and between Customers and supplier. They allow for the review of project goals, direction, and progress—and for redirection as required. They allow the project to move forward quickly and efficiently toward its goal of designing and developing high-quality T&D.

The Analysis Team

The Analysis Team is used to define performance requirements and enabling Knowledge and Skills.

The key responsibilities of the Analysis Team are to

- Provide input in analysis meetings regarding the missions, key outputs and metrics, tasks, and roles and responsibilities of ideal performance.
- Provide input in the analysis meetings regarding the typical gaps in performance (outputs not meeting

targeted metrics), likely causes of the gaps, and an assessment of the causes' root source being due to deficiencies in the environment, Knowledge/Skills/competencies, or physical and/or psychological attributes.

The Analysis Team usually has between 6 and 12 members (eight seems to be best). Less is hardly a team approach, and too many more becomes unwieldy in a group forum.

The Project Steering Team handpicks members of the Analysis Team, looking for:

- Mastery of performance
- Credibility with the Project Steering Team
- Credibility with the target audience they represent

This team is composed of members who can articulate the performance requirements of the job, task, or process. Collectively, team members will know all of the key enabling Knowledge and Skills.

They are themselves Master Performers or, minimally, Subject Matter Experts. Others who might make good Analysis Team members, depending on the situation, include managers and supervisors of the target audiences, and sometimes even novice performers.

Individual Master Performers are known for their *current* expertise in today's performance situation (not the knowledge they had three years ago before they took a headquarters staff job!). They have good reputations and are credible with their management and peers. They are often called upon to help others in the organization get out of trouble. They are often peer coaches for the organizations' novices. They usually have strong egos and strong personalities, and facilitating them can often be quite a challenge for ISD staff. If there are any limitations on who can be involved in the analysis process, choose these Master Performers! We benchmark them during the analysis process.

Subject Matter Experts are people who know a great deal about the job or some relevant issue, procedure, policy, tool, or problem. Subject Matter Experts may be knowledgeable about some aspect of performance or all of it; however, by the PACT definition they are not Master Performers unless they are currently performing a task to a level of mastery recognized by their own organization. Subject Matter Experts may *not* know how to get a job done when faced with today's real-world barriers and issues or how to work around or plow right through.

Manager and Supervisor Representatives are sometimes important. They often have the big picture when Master Performers and SMEs don't. For example, sometimes the near-term future state is being designed just one step ahead of the real work, and very few people may understand what's ahead in the future. This is often the result of past managerial practices of keeping most people in the dark, inadvertently or deliberately.

In any event, managers and supervisors are often placed in the PACT Processes and even deliberately invited to act as spies on behalf of the Project Steering Team.

Including **novice performers** is sometimes appropriate to the situation. While Master Performers are important because they have years of experience and understand the intricacies of performing the tasks on a daily basis, novice performers are important to the team because learning the job tasks has been a relatively recent experience to them.

Novice performers can identify critical sequencing, tasks, steps, and other information that is important in the eventual training; more experienced performers might take these aspects of the job for granted. Novice performers know which immediate survival skills are critical! If the focus of the project is on T&D for predominantly new hires, inclusion of these people may be especially useful.

Getting the right people into the right teams or roles is critical, but even if there are one or two ringers (people with really no business being involved except as political hacks), having a preponderance of the really right people balances everything out acceptably.

It *is* important to create an Analysis Team of diverse participants. Different folks add different perspectives to the analysis effort.

The Analysis Team ensures that real-world work performance, as documented in the Performance Model, becomes the ultimate criterion for the T&D's learning objectives. It also ensures that all additional analysis data, such as enabling Knowledge and Skills, is based on the Performance Model's description of ideal performance.

Teams versus Individuals

I have found that a team approach to conducting the analysis versus individual interviews and observations not only saves time, but it also creates an ownership by the participants in the results of the effort.

In reality, no one individual has all the information, and individual perceptions differ depending on experiences. By involving a mix of participants in the analysis processes, group synergies develop, resulting in analysis work products of much greater detail and accuracy.

But beware group think!

Guy W. Wallace

The Analysis Review Team

A team related to the Analysis Team is the Analysis Review Team. One or more Analysis Review Teams may be put in place to extend the review and buy-in of the analysis and design data.

Analysis Review Teams are formed when the Project Steering Team is worried that the small number of participants on the Analysis Team won't provide enough real-world input or won't cover the politics well enough geographically. The more diverse a large organization is, the more useful Analysis Review Teams may be.

For example, if Analysis Team members do not geographically represent the entire spectrum of target audience members, forming more broadly based Analysis Review Teams can provide valuable confirmation of the results obtained. Rather than overstaff the Analysis Team with the number sufficient to meet those concerns, slowing down the Analysis Team meeting, the PACT Process Project Manager should suggest the use of review teams.

Usually, these teams are created for political reasons. The efforts of these teams slow down processes and increase costs, but forming these teams is sometimes a necessity due to the politics and culture of the organization. They are not generally necessary when the Analysis Team and Design Team are staffed with the right people in the first place.

Participants on Analysis Review Teams include Master Performers, Subject Matter Experts, managers and supervisors, and novice performers. Analysis Review Team roles and responsibilities are similar in Curriculum Architecture Design, Modular Curriculum Development, and Instructional Activity Development.

Of Spies and Politics

Spies are necessary. We want them. (You would too, especially if you were the Project Steering Team chairperson.) So, of course, the Project Steering Team may need to plant their spies on the Design Team, too (politics again).

But think about it. When the spies report back the fact that the team accomplished its mission and produced good data, you've gone a long way toward survival and success in the political world. In fact, you could be a hero whose songs will soon be sung around the corporate campfires.

The Design Team

The Design Team is typically responsible for providing input in the design meeting regarding key content points, typical issues, level of detail required, estimates of time and length, and potential sources for the information.

In line with the saying that "The T&D Customer owns the *content*, and the T&D supplier owns the *process*," the Design Team is asked to contribute live, as they see the T&D design unfold before their eyes.

This is not *design by committee*; the Design Team does not do the design while the ISD practitioner sits and watches and writes. Rather, this is *influencing the Designer by committee;* the Designer designs T&D based on the analysis work products, doing that while Design Team members observe, critique, and contribute—live and on the spot.

As with the Analysis Team, the Project Steering Team handpicks the Design Team. The Design Team is composed of a subset of Analysis Team members, selected to represent all target audiences. Design Team members must

- Be team players.
- Be concrete thinkers as well as conceptual thinkers.
- Understand job performance and Knowledge/Skill requirements even better than Analysis Team members do.

Down-selecting Design Team members from the Analysis Team is a critical step. During the analysis meeting, the Project Manager and Analyst get a chance to see the personalities and styles of each member. That's when and how ISD professionals identify the best candidates for the next steps.

Why doesn't the Project Manager want *new* members on the Design Team? Analysis Team members have collectively worked their way through many decisions on job breakdowns, tasks, outputs, and so forth; they have organized the analysis data and should be comfortable and familiar with their organization.

New members struggle with this organization; they may feel the need to "fix" the analysis data before they can go ahead with the design process. Not only does this slow down the design process, it also makes the "old" Design Team members—the ones who served on the Analysis Team—upset because some newcomer is messing with "their" data.

During the Design Phase, the Project Manager can sometimes deflect a potential new member to a position on a Design Review Team rather than the Design Team.

But if it's absolutely necessary to add a new member to the Design Team, the Project Manager must make sure the new member becomes thoroughly familiar with the analysis data and its organization. This means walking the new member through the analysis outputs step by step, detail by detail, and enlightening him or her to how this data will be used downstream.

The Design Review Team

The Design Review Team is used to expand the involvement of the target audience and Stakeholders by having them critique the design effort's outputs. The rationale for having a Design Review Team is similar to the rationale for having an Analysis Review Team. Participants on a Design Review Team may represent any and all Stakeholders. The Design Review Team is a chance to have the design work products reviewed by members of the target audience and their managers.

The Development Team

The purpose of the Development Team is to help build the T&D designed in earlier parts of the PACT Processes. The Development Team is used in Modular Curriculum Development and Instructional Activity Development, but not Curriculum Architecture Design projects.

The purpose of the Development Team is to help draft and refine all instructional and pilot-test materials, following the guidelines of the design specs and maps.

The Development Team is composed of Master Performers and Subject Matter Experts who may or may not have been involved in the project earlier, typically as members of the Project Steering Team, Analysis Team, or Design Team. Development Team members work in conjunction with ISD Team members to build the T&D.

Development Team members are empowered to make minor modifications to the design, but they have to seek approval for any major changes. Development Team members may also have the additional responsibility of helping to deliver or administer the delivery of the T&D in initial pilot sessions or during deployment.

Subject Matter Experts and Master Performers are designated to fill the roles of

- Input Subject Matter Expert
- Review Subject Matter Expert
- Lead Subject Matter Expert

The **input Subject Matter Expert** assists in detailing the lesson outline, following the design specification. An instructional technologist is assigned to actually develop the lesson with the Subject Matter Expert's assistance.

The **review Subject Matter Expert** critiques lesson drafts; identifies additions, deletions, or corrections required; and submits all input and feedback to a lead Subject Matter Expert and the assigned developer.

The **lead Subject Matter Expert** is responsible for all T&D content in the modules and lessons they are assigned. Lead Subject Matter Experts integrate all T&D lesson materials as development proceeds. Lead Subject Matter Experts may also be lead facilitators for specific lessons.

Using the Development Team and the ISD Team, development—which includes micro-level analysis and design work—is finally accomplished in Phase 4 of Modular Curriculum Development or Instructional Activity Development. The micro-level analysis and design is thus deferred until T&D becomes a high priority and is resourced.

Along with the roles of facilitators and instructors, another role is crucial for the conduct of a pilot test: the role of the *pilot-test participants*. Participants attend and evaluate the initial delivery of the T&D for the purpose of generating evaluations and Revision Recommendations; the Project Steering Team considers these evaluations and recommendations.

Pilot-Test Team

Pilot-test participants are handpicked by the Project Steering Team to create a balance between

- Target Audience Representatives
- Management Representatives

Target Audience Representatives are from the pool of eventual learners who will participate in the T&D after the pilot. They are used to measure the amount of learning that occurs.

Management Representatives (a.k.a. management spies) are handpicked by the Project Steering Team to participate in the trial. They are used to determine whether the right learnings are taught. In combination, the two perspectives give the ISD Team the right data to determine what happened well and what did not.

Who Wants Spies?

T&D projects have long been fouled by management spies sent in for the first delivery. They attend to inspect and evaluate. They come out declaring that they really didn't learn much themselves.

Most of them may not have learned very much. But the design is usually not intended for the type of people who are normally sent in to spy and report back. The T&D is usually produced for the unknowing, those who can't tell you if it was the right stuff or not. But the unknowing *can* tell you if they learned anything at all, and it *can* be measured.

Management spies have always served management's need to ensure that the content in the T&D is good and appropriate before a general release is done for ongoing deployment. T&D's past reputation is not untarnished when it comes to the quality and worth of some of the products produced. Management always felt the need to "*inspect* quality in" because they were unsure the ISD process would "*build* quality in" from the beginning!

I always ask for both types of pilot participants, in close to equal numbers. When I rationalize my request to the Project Steering Team, I am almost always rewarded with the right mix. I lessen the chances that I won't get enough real learners compared to the real spies, so that it won't throw the pilot session into disarray when the spies claim *out loud* that this is below them, too simple, etc.

When target audience learners (some selected for their strength and ability to stand toe to toe with the wizened old veterans) declare, "Perhaps you forgot it was like when you were new," this shuts down the issue. At that point, the management spies might evaluate from a different, and more appropriate, perspective.

Chapter Summary & Transition

This chapter was intended to address the ISD Customer Teams and Roles for an MCD effort.

This chapter flows logically into the next about the knowledge and skills required for the ISD Team in their Role as an ISD team member dealing with \the ISD Customer's Teams and Roles, however your needs may have caused you to skip around the chapter sequence.

The following are the chapter titles and page numbers to assist you with your personal navigation needs.

Suggested Chapter Reflection & Reaction

I would suggest that prior to jumping into whichever chapter meets your needs that you give pause for a moment to reflect on the following and make some notes:

- Does this have applicability for me?

- What can I adopt from what I have read here?

- What are my potential needs for adaptation?

- What other issues do I see that I will need to address before embracing?

Please make note of your thoughts before proceeding.

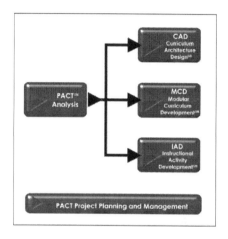

3 levels of ISD Methodologies
with common Analysis and
Project Planning & Management Methodologies.

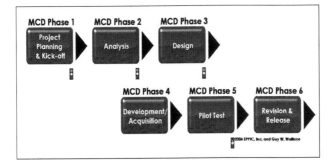

15 - MCD PRACTITIONER KNOWLEDGE AND SKILLS DEVELOPMENT

Chapter Overview

This chapter is intended to provide you with an overview of the key Knowledge and Skills required of ISD Supplier's

PACT Practitioners who will conduct CAD efforts, so that you might select candidates and then develop them.

Selection Guidelines

The PACT Processes are not for all ISD practitioners. Success in old ISD approaches and methods does not guarantee success with these new approaches and methodologies.

The key attributes required of PACT Processes Practitioners include the following:

- Knowledgeable of and experienced in ISD
- Skilled in group facilitation
- Strong personality but reasonable and flexible
- Able to think conceptually *and* concretely
- Skilled in presentation *and* listening
- Attentive to detail
- Broadly experienced through exposure to other jobs, departments, disciplines, and organizational functions

Being *detail oriented* seems to help a great deal, too.

Attributes that interfere with success in practicing the PACT Processes include:

- Poor group facilitation skills
- Timid personality
- Too much personal ego to allow Customers to own the content of the T&D
- Fear of making mistakes
- Overly cautious
- Slow to grasp concepts, patterns, and models
- Poor flip chart writing style (later no one can read or remember the content captured)

Non-ISD'ers who are bright, sharp, quick, and have strong group facilitation skills can become very successful PACT Practitioners. I have developed many who were new to ISD and became very successful with these methods.

In fact, because **PACT reduces ISD to practice**, it is actually easier sometimes to develop practitioners from outside the ISD community.

The real tricky parts are due to all of the facilitation of teams/ groups in the Group Processes for Analysis and Design.

The Group Analysis Process

It has often been noted that the people closest to the performance know what the issues are – and have a good idea about what it might take to solve them. Why not engage the best performers among them in the conduct of any analysis efforts?

Why force an Analyst to try to figure it out – when they could facilitate a group of knowledgeable performers and Stakeholders to make the determinations quicker, better and cheaper?

My professional affinity group has been talking and writing about teaching managers, supervisors and individual contributors our methods for performance improvement for decades. Teaching them to fish for themselves - so to speak.

This is my proxy for doing that. I know that once others have seen this process that many are capable of facilitating it to capture the data required. Of course, they need great facilitation skills.

The Group Process methods for analysis leverages those in the know about Performance – at the nuanced level – to first articulate ideal performance and call out any gaps and causes for those gaps.

After all – if I get the group of true Master Performers that I had asked for on my Analysis Team – they not only can be facilitated to help us capture what they know – and also what they've forgotten.

Most experts operate on auto–pilot for many of the things they do – and some research suggests that that can be up to 70% of what a novice needs to perform. They cannot tell you all of what's needed – one on one. But my experience since I started using groups is that they'll self-correct each other. Sometimes it is one-ups-men-ship – but most of the time it is simply great collaboration that they themselves see value in doing.

Master Performers also have great insight about those who are not Master Performers – for they often find themselves "bailing them out" as part of their job duties – in a manner of speaking. They know what's what when you're doing the Gap Analysis portion of the Performance Model.

The Group Process brings the Analysis Team together for an accelerated approach to analysis – as most entire jobs can be analyzed, producing Performance Models and Enabler Matrices in 2–3–4 days – depending on the scope of the performance to be analyzed, and the complexity, and the probable ease or difficulty in bring an assembled team to consensus.

Most of my MCD Analysis Meetings are two days. Some are 4. A few have been 5 – but I've never used more than 5 days to complete analysis of Performance and the enabling Knowledge/Skills.

Guy W. Wallace

Compare that 2-3-4 days to multiple weeks or months of analysis using the more traditional methods.

Clients would really prefer that we not take so long – and that we come back with a better-than-good understanding of their situation.

> I recall vividly a Client at Motorola, in 1981, telling me: I hate it when you guys come back 90 days later and tell us what we told you on day 1.

That's why most Clients will stop analysis from happening.

All too often we've subjected them to our methods which seems to them to lead to analysis paralysis – especially when the Clients "think" they know the root cause and the solution in the first place. They usually don't – but try convincing them of that without good data about a reasonably determined alternative root cause or causes!

> My approach is, "lets the chips of analysis data fall where they may. Let me quickly facilitate your handpicked Master Performers to see what consensus we can generate that describes the ideal state and the gaps of those not operating at a level of mastery.

> When they see that I want those folks for only 2-3-4 days – they usually buy it. After all – what can go wrong? Those Master Performers are usually handpicked for both their mastery and for their intolerance of analysis paralysis – they will want to get the data out as soon as possible! And they'll do it with high quality and relevance!

> Especially as I ask specifically for those tough qualities for intolerance of paralysis in those handpicked by the Clients in the selection process for the Master Performers.

The Group Process facilitator's job is to ensure the quality and quantity of the work products produced by the Analysis Team. For example, during the Analysis Team meeting the Group Process facilitator knows in advance how the outputs data will be organized, what kind of data is to be captured, and what analysis steps and questions will generate and enable capture of that key data quickly and efficiently.

The teams provide the inputs to the Process and ensure a consensus regarding the data (or flag the areas of dispute). Facilitation accelerates the progress of the team in generating a specific set of data in a specific format.

The Group Processes require a skillful facilitator to drive team Processes and later to conduct a project Gate Review Meeting with the Client. Without good facilitation skills, the Group Processes just will not work smoothly, effectively, or efficiently.

And the style of facilitation I've found to be most successful for the Group Process is different from some forms of "traditional" facilitation. The key difference between the facilitation for the Group Processes presented here and other types of Group Process facilitation is the amount of involvement and energy put forth by facilitators.

Group Process facilitators for these efforts need to be more proactive than reactive. They must *guide* the Process from the driver's seat and make things happen, rather than provide reflections from the back seat as the group meanders or drives itself. The facilitators are in control of the Process that involves the group; they are not bystanders there to comment on process or key issues they've observed.

The style of facilitation required for the Group Processes *is not* the more typical laid–back style of "sideline Process coaching." It is proactive, deliberate, driven, and leading (where appropriate).

In the Group Process **the facilitators "own the Process" while the team being facilitated "owns the Content**." That's why each party is on the payroll and in the room that particular day. That ownership needs to be made clear to everyone at the start and throughout – but that must be done carefully. Sometimes you can get a VERY negative reaction to that positioning – if you say that without the proper set up and "read" of the group.

The Group Process Facilitator Skills

The key attributes, values, knowledge, and skills required of the PACT Process facilitator are similar to the skills required of many facilitators. For example, a PACT Process facilitator must be a *good communicator*, able to

- Communicate well verbally
- Listen well
- Use the flip chart or electronic media effectively

The facilitator must be able to deal well with group dynamics. This means that he or she must be able to

- Negotiate smoothly and influence people
- Work well with diverse groups of people
- Handle group conflict

The facilitator has to have good problem–solving abilities. This means being

- Persistent
- Creative
- A systems thinker

- A conceptual thinker (versus literal)
- A strategic thinker (versus tactical)
- Able to suggest ideas
- Able to create models
- Able to work "bottom–up"
- Able to work "top–down"
- Able to deal with ambiguity
- Able to interpret data

And in addition, a good Group Process facilitator has a variety of other attributes, values, knowledge, and skills that come in handy. For example, the facilitator must be able to

- Be organized
- Handle details well
- Be decisive
- Deal with technical or unfamiliar content
- Appreciate diversity in ideas, people, etc.
- Appreciate the value of a common Process, where appropriate
- Appreciate Process management
- Flex Processes without sacrificing results

There are other Knowledge and Skills required, but these seem to be the really key ones.

12 Group Process Facilitation Guidelines

I call these "The 12 Rules and Guidelines of Proactive/ Confrontational Facilitation of the Group Processes."

They are:

1. Go Slow to Go Fast.
2. Be Declarative.
3. Write Stuff and Post It.

4. Be Redundant by Design.
5. Use the Four Key Communications Behavior Types.
6. Review and Preview.
7. Write It Down and Then Discuss It.
8. Use Humor.
9. Control the Process and the Participants.
10. Be Legible on the Flip Chart.
11. Beware of Group–Think.
12. Assign Parking Lot Valets.

Each of these is covered in more detail in the following text.

Read them. Adopt or Adapt them. And then use them.

1. Go Slow to Go Fast

Yikes! Go slow to go fast? We're almost always in a hurry and time is a wastin'.

Most time wasters in business meetings are due to the *hurry up* syndrome to which we typically let ourselves fall prey. "Just do it!" And then redo it. And, often enough to make us all dread meetings, redo it again!

The iterative nature of rework should cause us to stop and ponder just what the heck is going on and how we can stop it! We seem to be able to always find the time to redo work in most of those instances where we just couldn't seem to take the time to "do it right the first time."

We often forget to front–end load our meetings, to allow time at the beginning of a meeting to do what needs to be done up–front.

For example, we typically do a poor job in presenting, discussing, and rationalizing our ultimate objectives, our desired meeting outcomes, the meeting Process and methods we intend to employ, and the roles and responsibilities for each person in the Process, etc. We don't carefully get everyone on board before we take off. And then we pay dearly in costly, inefficient work and the downstream rework.

We seem to feel that because we (or someone else) said it once, and therefore the intent of the message was sufficiently conveyed, that we're done with that and it's time to do the deep dive and get on with it! Yikes is right.

Slow down! Sloowww waaaaayyyyy doooowwwwnnnnnnnn.

The slower you go in your meeting start–up mode, the quicker you'll get to your termination point with the right stuff. The more time spent on ensuring that all of the participants—who each brought their own personalized styles and capabilities, thank you very much—get themselves mentally on board with your agenda and concede to it, the sooner your train will get to where it's going.

When I go slowly, it's to do an orientation, cover the big picture, etc. This is sometimes called the "advance organizer." Use it! Get everyone's mental model closer to yours, or let them push back and then get yours closer to theirs.

Once done you can "rocket and roll"—up to the next transition point that is, which is a new Process or a new day. Then it's slow down, take your time, and when the time is right, rocket and roll again!

To kick off a meeting, I like to cover the *overall project purpose and objectives* first—the terminal objective, if you will. I like to cover the *specific meeting purpose and objectives* next, and ensure that everyone sees the link between the two. The specific meeting purpose and objectives are Enablers for the terminal objective and should be seen as such.

Then if there are other meetings and Processes that all fit into the big picture of the project (which almost always depends on its scope, etc.), I cover them also, so everyone sees what we will be doing and how it fits with everything else. Start looking into the participants' eyes to look for clues and cues of understanding or confusion, acceptance or rejection.

If some other group or Process is going to tackle other project steps and Enablers, my group needs to understand the intent of the project's plan: who's on first, on second, and which group is up to bat, etc. I like everyone to know not only what's *in* our "box" but what's *outside* our box. Clarify so that everyone can build their own mental model. Draw a diagram if you can.

All of this front–end preparation takes time. *Go slow to go fast.* You'll be surprised at how fast you can actually go if you don't have to keep slowing down to revisit topics and issues already covered.

You'll also need to slow down when you transition from one part of your meeting to the next; for example, going from performance modeling to enabler analysis.

Again, explain how this next Process fits. Look for the clues and cues in participants' eyes and body language. Most importantly, ask participants whether they understand or not. If you don't ask, they might not tell you.

At the start of a new day I do the same thing, go slow to go fast. I call these transitions "reviews and previews." More on these later.

2. Be Declarative

The timid shall never inherit the Master Performer facilitator's crown.

Be strong. If your job is to facilitate a Process to a certain set of outcomes, then declare yourself to the group. Tell them (assuming you *are* in charge of the meeting and the Process and *are* responsible for assisting in getting the group outputs out) what's what and who's who. Describe the Process and the products of your Process. Declare your intentions!

Tell the group what they will do, how you plan to get them there, which hoops you'll collectively be jumping through, which ones are on fire, etc. *Be declarative*! Then, as you start and throughout your Process, ask for feedback, because there may indeed be a better way, or what you want may already exist, etc.

Do plenty of *Process checks*. Ask, "So far, so good? Does this make any sense to you because even though it looks good to me, what do I know? I'm just the facilitator here."

Be declarative about wanting and demanding their feedback. After all, that is why they are on the payroll this day: to participate fully in the Process.

I tell 'em what I want, how I intend for us to go about doing it, and then I ask for their "questions/ comments/ concerns" in return. Heck, I *beg* for their feedback! I ask them to "shoot a warning shot across my bow" (a residue phrase from my days in the U. S. Navy).

I plead that they please don't let me drive us collectively down a blind alley on a dead–end street! I may have a plan and firmly declare my intentions, but I'm still open to the warnings of others.

Hey, I've been *burned* before, and I have *learned* from it. I've learned to get group input and feedback. This concept is not new. It's nothing more than lessons gleaned from project postmortems—where Project Managers realized that the people in their projects saw the bad news on the horizon long before it arrived to screw up their projects. If only the Project Managers had asked earlier or had known whom to ask! Your project participants may see the problematic issues long before you see them. They may know that the light up ahead is not the end of the tunnel, but a freight train coming!

Be declarative and see what happens. If not much happens, don't assume that you are cool and okay. Double– and triple–check with the group. And look for those nonverbal clues and cues that something is amiss!

WARNING! Sometimes you may come on so strong in your "facilitator declarative mode" that members of the group may feel a bit intimidated and unwilling to suggest things or challenge you. You must ensure that the group always feels as if they truly *own the content* and that you only *own the Process*.

This declarative stuff is a double–edged sword—it cuts *both* ways. Be careful! A skilled facilitator carefully maneuvers a group through a Process using both strong and gentle pushes and pulls, all the while remaining focused on the desired outcomes.

3. Write Stuff and Post It

Regardless of whether it's words, diagrams, or charts that can best capture the essence of the team conversation, just don't stand around while people (including you) are talking. Write it or chart it on flip chart paper or on electronic media and *make it visible!*

Put it in black and white (or color if that helps) so that everyone can *see* what it is that we're discussing. Give them something to think about and react to.

If you let participant input remain as nebulous thoughts floating about the room, you have not given others a chance to visualize, self–inspect, critique, and fix what it is they are talking about.

Make it visual. Make it visible! Don't bury it by flipping to a new clean page. Rip it off and post it! Keep everything visible.

4. Be Redundant by Design

All marketers know that for a message to penetrate the psyche of the receiver and convey the intent of the message, it will need to be repeated . . . and repeated . . . and repeated.

Enough said? I don't think so. If you've said it once, you'll probably need to repeat it.

This becomes a problem for those who are quicker on the uptake. Just as group–paced, traditional training is usually held hostage by the slowest in the group, so too are meetings. Those who get it quicker will get irritated with you for thinking they didn't get it sooner. This is tricky.

Who do you play to: the quick or the slow? I play to the slow. If I sense that some individuals are getting annoyed with me for this, I talk with them on break and enlist them in my efforts to get everyone else on board. They are usually *way cool* with it, because they're in on it and know that I know it's not them! (I told you this was tricky!)

Usually they will step in during my next bout of "redundantitis," and help me explain my point. Often they have a better command of the group's language and jargon and can provide better examples, non–examples, and analogies that may actually cause the cognitive breakthrough I was struggling to create. The whole group breathes a collective sigh of relief when they all get it or know that everyone else has finally gotten it and that I will quit beating them over the head with it.

I could let my own ego get in the way and not create the tension that *redundancy by design* causes by saying it once and moving on. But having been burned by that, I have learned to face the short–term wrath of the group in order to ensure that the train is moving ahead with everyone on board.

Also, some of your Clients may feel that since they get it, everyone else must have as well. They may make the mistake of thinking that your redundancy is no longer tolerable because they see the quicker "learners" of the group squirming. But they often aren't often in a position to read the clues and cues in everyone's eyes as you are from center stage. Balancing the Clients' needs to keep the group happy and see progress without getting impatient and moving on too quickly can be tricky.

You'll need to determine when it's safest to proceed—when you can leave someone behind conceptually. When will it do little or great damage to your next steps? Will it cause problems in these next steps, will it cause rework, will it cause greater frustration in the rest of the group, will it then destroy any group "team–ness" that may be starting to form? Tricky, eh?

5. Use the Four Key Communications Behavior Types

The single most powerful insight I have gained in my evolution as a facilitator was from my exposure to a "communications behavioral model" from a "Win–Win

Negotiating" course and a "SPIN®" sales training course from Neil Rackham of Huthwaite, Inc. I feel most fortunate to have been involved in those courses in 1981 while I was at Motorola Training & Education Center (MTEC—the forerunner of Motorola University).

The model identifies four key verbal communications behaviors. I almost always categorize my verbal expressions into these four, even as I say them. And I typically "see" others' verbal expressions falling into these categories, even as they speak!

The four types are

1. Giving Information
2. Seeking Information
3. Testing·Understanding/ Summarizing
4. Defend/ Attack

Giving Information

The "giving information" communications behavior is straightforward and important. When facilitating the Group Analysis Process, giving information is the place to begin. Generally, you may need to first *give* some information before you "find things out," but you should soon be shifting gears into the next type.

Seeking Information

The "seeking information" communications behavior also is simple. It's typically in question form, either open–ended or closed–ended, depending on what you're trying to accomplish.

Knowing how you balance these first two types of communications behaviors is important in assessing your success and failure as a communicator, but nothing beats the next communication behaviors.

Testing Understanding/ Summarizing

The "testing understanding/ summarizing" is actually a combination of two behaviors, but I often combine them to simplify their use. However, they *are* different.

Testing understanding is making statements or asking questions for the purpose of testing what you think you've just heard or what you think you know. Most of us know this as a form of "active listening."

One of the best ways to test understanding is to paraphrase what was said. Putting it into another set of words, rather than simply parroting it back just as you heard it, allows the sender to better check your receipt of their message. If you parrot it back, all we know is that you remembered the words. The further your paraphrasing takes your words away from the words originally used, the easier it is for you to test for your understanding. And helping others to a better understanding as well.

It is also best to be somewhat declarative of what you're doing when you test understanding. I often announce, "I am testing here" and then make a statement or ask a question. Then listen for the response, and always read the clues and cues of nonverbal facial and body language. You can also say, "Let me see if I've got this. You're saying that x, y, and then z. Is that right?"

Work on your own set of phrases to test understanding. Play with it!

The second part of this behavior is *summarizing*. Again, it's best to provide your own clues and cues to your group. Say, "Let me try to summarize this," and then do it. If your words stray from the original (but not too far), then it's easier for the group to react.

Summarizing is very much like testing understanding, just done in a different mode. You are looking for feedback from the group that you are either right on, just off, or way off. Again, don't let your ego get in the way! I tell groups, "As a facilitator, I can't be afraid to be wrong because it'll slow us down. In fact, I'm often wrong. So get used to it! Your job here today is also to correct me and keep me on the straight and narrow Path!"

Testing understanding and summarizing are critical to ensure that we understand the meanings behind the words that others are using. As a colleague of mine once remarked: "It not just semantics, it's *always* semantics!"

Testing understanding and summarizing helps we receivers comprehend the intent of the message sender. Testing understanding can be a very powerful tool for a facilitator.

Of course, Socrates used this technique way back when, so be careful! Watch out for hemlock.

Defend/ Attack

The "Defend/ Attack" behavior is also a combination. Defending is typically in response to a real or perceived attack. No matter how it starts, it usually degenerates into a defend/ attack spiral that won't end until someone interrupts the spiral.

The best interruption is to test understanding and summarize—something on the order of, "So you're saying that this proactive facilitator stuff is just a bunch of hooey, and that the author must be a real jerk to perpetuate this garbage by committing it to paper and then disseminating it to the public?"

Usually a short string of tests and summaries are sufficient to defuse the situation and end a defend/ attack spiral. All that the irate person usually wants is to be heard (and understood). Get the conversation back to more civilized ground and reduce the heat.

In my mind, the power of testing understanding and summarizing cannot be underestimated. Try it yourself. Try it on the kids. Try it with your significant other. (But stay away from gang fights!)

Using the Four Key Communications Behavior Types

The four types are:

1. Giving Information
2. Seeking Information
3. Testing Understanding/ Summarizing
4. Defend/ Attack

Once I learned the four communications behavior types, I began to "see" all of my own verbal utterings as falling into one of the four categories.

I learned to first give information, maybe a little or a bunch, and then to soon test understanding. Do they get it? For example, "I want us to list all of the outputs for this Area of Performance and then identify all of the key measures of performance for each. Are we all clear on what I mean by performance outputs?"

Or, "We need to identify the typical performance gaps, if any, for this output."

Or, in response to the group's input, I test understanding for my benefit. "So the typical gap is that they are almost always late in turning in the monthly report?"

I also test understanding in response to their statements. "Let me test this out. You're saying that there are indeed typical gaps, but they don't sync up with any of the key measures we have currently listed."

I learned to seek information and then summarize. "What gaps do you think there are, and what key output measures would reflect those gaps?" I would respond to their response with, "So we seem to be saying that it would be both a time to complete as well as a timeliness measure."

I learned that the best way to break a defend/ attack spiral is to first test understanding/ summarize and then either give information or seek information. "So you think that global IT dropped the ball and didn't get the vendor into the effort soon enough, driving up your costs due to all of the overtime that was incurred trying to catch up?"

I learned that the more I test understanding and summarize the more it benefits the group, because they are sometimes hesitant to appear slow. Again, I can't afford to let my own ego get in the way of potentially appearing confused, slow, etc. I've learned that the really smart people in the room will quickly figure me out and that I won't appear slow at all, no matter how hard I might appear to be trying with all of this testing understanding behavior.

This is great stuff. It made me more comfortable to have these communication behavioral tools at my disposal when I first started, and I believe it has made a big difference in my approach and style. It has made me a much better facilitator.

6. Review and Preview

I start with a "review/ preview" at the beginning of every new day of a multiday meeting, at any mid–meeting Process change, and at the return from every meeting break. Some might call it a progress check. "How are we doing, is everyone comfortable with what we have captured, etc.?"

I do that within the context of "where have we been, and where are we going." I like to think of it as "recalibrating" the group. They are often simply along for the ride, and sometimes they are just not that interested in learning the Process we are using, so they often forget the Process (often to the facilitator's amazement). But hey, this is our world—this facilitation stuff—not theirs. So I need a way to remind them continuously of what we are doing and where we are going and how it all fits together.

Participants may do very well in responding to our prompts, giving us their feedback when asked. But do not be fooled into believing that after one, two, or even three days they will remember exactly how and why we did each step of our Process.

Our model for capturing and analyzing data is probably somewhat alien to them. It's often very different from their personal mental model of how we facilitators should be doing our job. They often play along with us without completely giving up their mental model. They may still be quite comfortable with theirs and not with the new one just emerging.

I find that groups often revert midstream to something else (I often know not what), and I need to recalibrate the group to the Process we are using. In fact, I try to do it before it really becomes apparent that it is needed (by looking for those cues and clues!).

Reviewing and previewing gives me a chance to recalibrate the group, re–establish the models and terms, and just as importantly, give the group a place to blow off any steam or frustrations that may exist.

Blowing off steam is critical. If the group needs an outlet, they'll either do it on your schedule or when, in the immortal words of Popeye, "They can't stands it no more." You should have seen it coming, in the clues and cues for which you are constantly looking. The reviews and previews are a safety outlet designed into my Process checks.

"Please do it now and be less disruptive to the main Process," I think. The reviews/ previews are the time and place for blowing off steam and airing any and all frustrations. Remember, it's either done on your schedule or theirs. You can try to stop it, but I bet you often won't be able to stop it at all. You may only make it worse. You may be able to control this to your advantage, but only if you try. It is often (but not always) yours to control.

Think of this "review/ preview" as a combination of

- Slowing down temporarily in order to go fast again
- Being declarative
- Redundancy by design
- A progress/ Process check

Don't be afraid to do this several times a day and at the beginning and ending of each day. The review should cover our project purpose, meeting purpose, outputs/ outcomes so far, and feedback and inputs. The preview covers where we are, where we are going, how we're progressing against the clock (are we on schedule or not?), and how the remaining agenda items fit into the overall scheme of things.

7. Write It Down and then Discuss It

One of my golden rules or guidelines to new facilitators is: Write down the first thing that someone says!

Turn words floating in the air into something black and white – depending, of course, on your paper and pen color. This almost always forces a reaction from the remaining members of the group you are facilitating.

I always tell the group that this is exactly what I'm going to do. If someone will be so brave as to volunteer a response to my question or statement, I'll write it down to prompt their reaction. Either it stays, or someone takes exception to it and the group dialogue begins. Do we have a consensus or not? Until I write it down, I'm not always sure. It's the reaction of the group, verbally or nonverbally (those clues and cues again), that tell me.

I tell the group that today they are on the payroll to provide the inputs according to my Process. They should all be okay with not being in total agreement, and they must be okay with questioning and challenging each other. We are usually in a hurry and need to accomplish plenty, and time is a wastin'. The best way to keep the Process moving is to seek what you're looking for, write down the first response, and then ask for group confirmation, questions, comments, and concerns.

If the facilitator asks and then does nothing with the response, he or she seems to be waiting for the correct answer. That tends to inhibit the free flow of responses that you may be seeking. I always write the response down, unless it is *so wrong* that I don't want to overly embarrass the individual who volunteered the wrong stuff. Then I rephrase my question so drastically, or shift gears and go into something that I may have forgotten, and then ask again usually with an example or two of what I'm looking for.

Of course some may know exactly what I've done and will usually appreciate it. They bet that if they make a similar *faux pas*, I'll help save their face, too. This fear–reduction technique is especially important when the group being facilitated is not totally comfortable with each other.

Again, this is not passive facilitation, which might be the appropriate route to take for your facilitation assignment for some other purpose.

This is aggressive, confrontational, proactive facilitation. This is the quickest route to getting the most data out of a Group Process. You need to decide the appropriateness of this method for your needs and for your personality style.

8. Use Humor

Humor, done right, sets the stage. The message sent by humor (and which can also be said out loud in a *declarative* fashion) is that while our goal is serious, let's not take ourselves too seriously. Let's loosen up a bit.

Self–deprecating humor is best. It offends no one, because you (the facilitator) are the butt of most of it or all of it.

Use of yourself as the "bozo on the bus" is effective because you can make points and laugh at yourself. And if you later inadvertently make someone else the butt of your jokes or points, you can recover by turning it back on yourself. For example: "Oh, that was smart . . . I guess you're joining me in the *duh–uh* club. Hey, but I'm still the president and/ or head clown."

When providing examples and non–examples, use yourself as the non–example and others in the room as the example. "Joey is competent and will get the assignment, and if he does well, he'll get the raise. Guy is still screwing up, and if the assignment doesn't go well, well he's outta here!"

Don't use off–color humor, sexist, racist, age–ist, or any non–PC (politically correct) humor. Make sure the butt of your jokes is most often you. Who could complain if you don't use off–color humor, sexist, racist, age–ist humor?

After establishing myself as the biggest bozo on the bus, I often include others in my other jokes/ wisecracks—but only if I am *darn sure* that they'll be okay with it, for example because they have started picking on me (in fun of course), or they have made fun of themselves in some way. Again, this is tricky and you've got to be sure of what you're doing.

If humor doesn't come naturally to you, try this first at your next family outing before you attempt to foist any humor on a group or team you are asked to facilitate. See what kind of reaction you get (from people who know you and love you much better than this possible group of strangers who won't be quite sure where you're coming from).

9. Control the Process and the Participants

The facilitator can never let one individual, or a small group within the larger group, dominate the meeting.

The best thing to do if this begins to happen to you is to thank the person for their input and then ask someone else for theirs. Then shift your style to aim specific questions at specific individuals. "Bob, what do you think the next set of tasks are for this output?"

Take the offenders aside at the next break and explain that you need a balance of inputs to ensure a consensus is forming. While you appreciate their contributions, you hope they understand what you're doing. Usually they get the message and back off. Maybe they'll need another reminder or two. Sometimes none of these tactics work.

It is rare, but I have "disinvited" participants from my meetings. That means I've been at the point that their participation was so dysfunctional that I asked them to leave. When they resisted, I suggested that I would call their boss to insist that they be requested to return to the office. That's when they either drastically changed their behavior, or they left. I had no choice. They were so disruptive that they were wasting the time and productivity of everyone else.

Of course, I'd given the disruptive participants plenty of warning. Prior to dismissing them, I had taken them aside during a specially called break and warned them of my next move (which would be insisting that they depart the Process). Prior to *that* I had taken them aside during a regular break to discuss their participation style and the effect on the group and our progress. Prior to that I had tried to manage their behavior during the meeting by asking out loud that they let others participate more. Prior to that I had tried to get the group to help me self–manage the problem participant by asking for their opinions in response to the one individual's points.

I had exhausted all possibilities. I had tried, I was done, and so were they.

When push comes to shove, I have to shove back. I am the person that the group looks to to control the Process and continue our progress. I can't blame their hesitancy to act. Otherwise, I am allowing someone (or more than one person) to waste all of our collective time and energies.

Don't let this happen to you. Take charge, take action. It isn't pleasant, but it *is* the job of the facilitator—at least in my view of the role of the proactive facilitator.

10. Be Legible on the Flip Chart

Another of my favorite rules is: "Neatness does not count; legibility does."

Maybe it just suits my personality best, being somewhat messy. Those who know me usually think differently. I'm a very structured person—I love structure and hate chaos. But once I get on a roll with the group, or more importantly, once they get on a roll, I don't take a lot of time to write down their inputs so carefully that I slow them down. I try to write fast.

In fact, I write so fast and furiously that I have to make sure I don't violate the legibility rule that means so much to whoever has to word–Process my work afterward. Even when I have word–Processed my charts later, I have found that I was not always able to recall what the words were in my attempt to clean up my own mess.

So if you can't do both quickly, at least be legible if not always neat when being fast!

11. Beware of Group–Think

Group–think is a danger. It is usually caused by one or more variables.

- A single dominant participant who intimidates everyone else, such as a high–level manager to whom most everyone else in the room reports to
- Multiple dominant participants who are aligned
- A docile, lazy group easily dominated and that

doesn't want to work too hard
- A group of timid participants, unsure of themselves, and afraid of going against the grain of the stronger personalities

The key root cause could be poor selection of the group members for the meeting. This is sometimes avoidable and sometimes it is not.

It is more likely that group–think is caused by a facilitator who has lost control of the Process and has let someone else facilitate from the other side of the U–shaped tables. Bad. Bad. Bad.

When I feel that group–think is happening, I stop the Process and confront the group. I ask them to go over their last inputs and give me their personal rationale for their decisions. I tell them (being *declarative* of course) of my concern and ask them to speak for themselves. Then I back up and go over the last inputs very slowly, and reconfirm their responses and their rationale. If that doesn't stop it, maybe nothing will, unless we change the entire nature of the group Process.

It may be avoided initially by making sure that the folks chosen for the group effort are strong enough to not fall into the group–think trap.

12. Assign Parking Lot Valets

In a very structured Process, it's a good idea to use a "parking lot" for issues that may not be timely. Post a flip chart on the wall and write "Issue Parking Lot" or something similar on the top, and then add things that are premature, that we don't intend to address in the meeting, or that we don't want to forget. At the end of the meeting, or sooner as appropriate, address them and close them out.

Those that remain open will have to be addressed and resolved some other time and some other way.

I usually have two parking lots, one for open issues and one for closed issues, so everyone can see progress in addressing those that *can be* addressed in our meeting.

But I hate being the parking valet! It seems that I spend so much time parking everyone's issues that I run myself ragged from one flip chart to another. So I've hit on this device—an improvement if you will.

We hand out "stickies" and ask everyone to jot down their own issues and self–park them. Then at every review/ preview checkpoint, we review what's new in the open parking lot, and we take the time to see what can be parked in the other lot.

Try it. It gets your group more involved, makes them articulate their issues themselves, and gets them out of their seats on occasion, which may be the most beneficial aspect of the self–parking lot concept.

Other Skills for Your Toolkit

I've covered many of the facilitation styles and skills required for conducting Group Process Analysis Team meetings. But being a successful facilitator requires other Knowledge and Skills. Some of those include having a command of the following mini–Processes, often used within larger Processes and sometimes used by themselves. The ones that I've found key for my repertoire include

- Process modeling or mapping
- Systematic problem solving
- Systematic root cause analysis

- Systematic decision–making
- Systematic and systems thinking in general

Chapter Summary & Transition

This chapter was intended to address the Knowledge and Skills an MCD Practitioner needs to have or develop.

This chapter flows logically into the next, however your needs may cause you to want to skip around.

The following are the chapter titles and page numbers to assist you with your personal navigation needs.

Suggested Chapter Reflection & Reaction

I would suggest that prior to jumping into whichever chapter meets your needs that you give pause for a moment to reflect on the following and make some notes:

- Does this have applicability for me?

- What can I adopt from what I have read here?

- What are my potential needs for adaptation?

- What other issues do I see that I will need to address before embracing?

Please make note of your thoughts before proceeding.

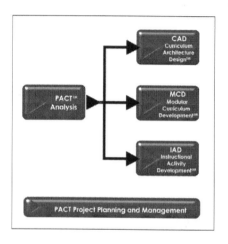

3 levels of ISD Methodologies
with common Analysis and
Project Planning & Management Methodologies.

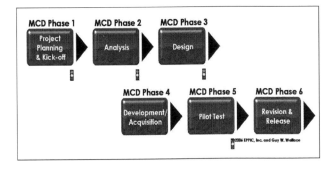

16 – OTHER USES FOR THE ANALYSIS DATA AND DATA ANALYSIS EXTENSION

Chapter Overview

This chapter is intended to provide you examples for uses of the analysis data beyond ISD – and what extensions of the data-set described here in this book for ISD efforts that you may need to make.

Additional Uses of PACT Data

A benefit of the PACT analysis methodologies is that analysis data has many other potential uses. For example, with a few modifications, the process can be used to augment an organization's business process modeling for a Total Quality Management continuous improvement effort.

Once the dEs (environmental deficiencies) are identified, it's up to management (the Project Steering Team) to decide to address them – or live with them.

Remember the words of the late Edward Deming, the renown quality guru of the '80s and '90s in the United States (and in the '50s and '60s in Japan): "Eighty percent of all quality problems are in the control of management."

Other additional analysis efforts might include the articulation of the various human *attributes and values* required for high performance. The Performance Model provides information from which physical, psychological, and intellectual requirements can also be derived. These may then lead to the creation or updating of a selection system, an assessment system, or a Performance Management System.

The Performance Model and Knowledge/Skill Matrix can provide information on how to make hiring decisions. For example, should we hire people with certain skills or should we provide training to get them?

PACT analysis data can provide the information necessary to run a performance management system. These systems may be used for assessment of qualification, for certification, or simply as part of the annual compensation review and adjustment drill. The data can also be used to set up very structured pay for Knowledge/Skill compensation systems.

The **graphic on the next page** portrays other uses for PACT analysis data. These include defining the requirements for the systems in place in an Enterprise that provide the human and environmental assets required by the processes ~ Performance Competence requirements as defined by the Performance Models covered in detail in chapter 7.

All of these downstream uses for the Performance Model data can have tremendous value to an enterprise seeking high performance.

The Processes

The Processes themselves might be what needs to be addressed – versus training for the performers.

The data in the Performance Models might suggest exactly where and what needs to be "fixed" – as many of the Master Performers probably commented on during the generation of that data.

Or it could be that the process is fine – and that it's the enablers of the process that need attending to.

Those enablers are the Environmental Assets and the Human Assets. But if they are deficient – one must look to the internal or external processes that provision those to the processes inadequately – and fix those.

Addressing all of this is beyond the scope of this book, but let's overview those now.

Process Performance & Enabler Analysis
Organization & Job Redesign Systems
Staffing & Succession Planning Systems
Recruiting & Selection Systems
Training & Development Systems
Performance Appraisal & Management Systems
Compensation & Benefits Systems
Reward & Recognition Systems
Information & Data Systems
Materials & Supplies Systems
Tools & Equipment Systems
Financial Systems
Facilities & Grounds Systems
Culture & Consequence Systems

The Environmental Assets

A Process needs the following non–human assets to operate and produce the Outputs it was designed to produce. These non–human assets – the Environmental Assets – include:

- Information/ data
- Tools/ equipment
- Materials/ supplies
- Facilities/ grounds
- Budget/ headcount
- Consequences (+/ –)

The provisioning systems – those internal Enterprise entities or systems – or external systems – that provide these to the Process – are presented next.

The 6 systems within the **Environmental Asset Management System** are:

1. Data & Information Systems
2. Materials & Supplies Systems
3. Tools & Equipment Systems
4. Facilities & Grounds Systems
5. Financial Systems
6. Culture & Consequence Systems

Here is a quick overview of each of the 6.

Data and Information Systems

The Data & Information Systems provide a wide variety of data and information, such as business strategies, competitive insights, work orders, results data, etc., needed to enable job holders to perform at a level of Performance Competence.

Material and Supply Systems

The Materials & Supplies Systems provide all of the materials and supplies needed to enable job holders to perform at a level of Performance Competence. These can include consumables used in the Process to produce Outputs and elements of the final Output for the Products and/ or Services resulting from the Processes.

Tool and Equipment Systems

The Tools & Equipment Systems provide the tools, equipment, machinery, and vehicles needed to enable job holders to perform at a level of Performance Competence. Perhaps the Process requires a fork-lift – or a new IT system.

Facilities/ Grounds Systems

The Facilities & Grounds Systems provide the buildings, grounds and other facilities, such as utilities for communications/ power/ water/ etc. that are needed to enable jobholders to perform at a level of Performance Competence. Some Process efforts need a "clean room" and others can be done outdoors in a parking lot – or on a test track.

Financial Systems

The Financial Systems provide the capital and expense budgets, and the headcount budgets needed to enable and support job holders in performing at a level of Performance Competence. Money is the grease of many Processes – if not all.

Culture and Consequences Systems

The Culture & Consequence Systems reinforce Enterprise cultural norms, and ensures that all of the management reinforcements (and extinguishments) needed are in place to encourage (or discourage) and enable job holders to perform at a level of Performance Competence.

I contend that Culture is the Consequences – or rather, is the result of the Consequence System.

Summary – Environmental Assets Management Systems

Way back in the day, a cavewomen had a job to do – a Process to do. There were Performance Competence Requirements – even back then.

Before she showed up to the cave – the environmental assets were either there or nearby in adequate quality and quantity for her use – or they were not. She may have needed food stuff, a rock bowl or plate, sticks for hanging the meat over the fire – and fire – in a fire pit that won't allow the wind to extinguish the fire.

The provisioning systems as I call them, won't appear on any organization chart named or configured this way.

You'll have to conduct additional analysis later on to figure out exactly where they are inside your Enterprise – and how many different organizational entities do this kind of provisioning to the Processes.

The key questions for you are:

- Are the Environmental Assets available adequate to the needs of the Process or Processes?
- Might the systems that provide these be subject to change for the purposes of improving their Processes to enable Performance Competence of your targeted Processes?

Next we'll overview the Human Asset Enablers and the systems that organize, obtain, maintain and provision those assets to the Processes.

The Human Assets

The Humans involved in any Process need the "right stuff" to work with/ manipulate the Environmental Assets in concert with the Processes' specific needs.

The Human Assets themselves are:

- Awareness, knowledge, skills
- Physical attributes
- Psychological attributes
- Intellectual attributes
- Values

Those assets are what the humans bring to the party – so to speak.

The 7 **Human Asset Management Systems** that organize, obtain, develop and maintain Human Assets – or "humans as assets," follow.

These systems generally determine and provision humans with the "right stuff" in support of the Processes, in concert with the Processes' specific needs.

The Human Asset Management Systems include:

1. Organization & Job Design Systems
2. Staffing & Succession Systems
3. Recruiting & Selection Systems
4. Training & Development Systems

5. Performance Appraisal & Management Systems
6. Compensation & Benefits Systems
7. Rewards & Recognition Systems

Let's quickly overview each of these.

Job and Organization Design Systems
The Organization & Job Redesign Systems provide a set of job designs and an organization design conducive to the needs of the Process, and its current and future volumes of work effort – and to the likely Human Assets available.

If you often need a "switch hitter" for baseball – someone who can bat from the right and left sides of home plate as needed - but you cannot find them in sufficient quantities – you'll need to change the organization and job design. The same if your Process requires both conceptual and concrete thinkers. Perhaps that requires two jobs rather than one.

Staffing and Succession Planning Systems
Staffing & Succession Systems provide the strategies, plans and mechanisms for developing a staffing plan and succession strategies. This may be important for the recruiting and retention of people now – as well as for the long term growth needs of the Enterprise.

Selection and Recruiting Systems
The Recruiting & Selection Systems provide the strategies, plans and mechanisms for first recruiting and then selecting the best candidates in the right quantities – from inside or outside the Enterprise.

Training and Development Systems
The Training & Development Systems provide the strategies, plans and mechanisms to train and develop the new hires and incumbents consistent with their Processes'

Performance Competence Requirements, now and in the future.

Performance Appraisal and Management Changes

The Performance Appraisal & Management Systems provide the strategies, plans and mechanisms for appraising job task performance and managing all "performance" issues via feedback, training and development and/ or progressive discipline.

Compensation and Benefits Systems

The Compensation & Benefits Systems provide the strategies, plans and mechanisms to ensure that the total pay and benefits offered attracts and retains competent staff.

Rewards and Recognition Systems

The Rewards & Recognition Systems provide the strategies, plans and mechanisms for providing non–monetary and small–monetary rewards and recognition.

Summary – Human Assets Management Systems

That cavewoman introduced earlier either knows what to do or has the skills for how to perform – with the Environmental Assets available in the cave – or she does not. She either has the physical attributes, the psychological and intellectual attributes to do the job – as well as the values needed – or she does not.

If she is lacking any of these, perhaps the female elders of the tribe will need to reconfigure her job task assignments to take advantage of her unique capabilities – or lack thereof. Or assign her other tasks.

The provisioning systems as I call them, won't appear on any organization chart named or configured this way – although a Human Resources organization typically has a role in many of these.

You'll have to conduct additional analysis later on to figure out exactly where they are inside your Enterprise – and how many different organizational entities do this kind of provisioning to the Processes.

The key questions for you are:

- Are the Human Assets available adequate to the needs of the Process or Processes?
- Might the systems that provide these be subject to change for the purposes of improving their own Processes to enable Performance Competence to your targeted Processes?

Data Extensions

Human Assets Requirements Data
The data regarding the Human Assets that you would need to redesign the Human Asset Management Systems includes:

- Awareness, knowledge, skills
- Physical attributes
- Psychological attributes
- Intellectual attributes
- Values

The ISD data only includes the "Awareness, knowledge, skills" – so this would need to be included in additional analysis efforts.

Think of additional Enabler Matrices – with perhaps another layer of categories – such as the 17 Categories of K/S presented earlier in chapter 7.

Environmental Assets Requirements Data

A Process and the humans performing in the process also need the following non–human/environmental assets to operate and produce the Outputs that the Process was designed to produce.

These non–human assets – the Environmental Assets – include:

- Information/ data
- Tools/ equipment
- Materials/ supplies
- Facilities/ grounds
- Budget/ headcount
- Consequences (+/ –)

Think of additional Enabler Matrices – with perhaps another layer of categories – such as the 17 Categories of K/S presented earlier in chapter 7, for these Environmental Assets.

Chapter Summary & Transition

This chapter was intended to intended to provide you examples for uses of the analysis data beyond ISD – and what extensions of the data-set described here in this book for ISD efforts that you may need to make.

This chapter leads to the summary and close of the book.

Your needs may have caused you to skip around and read these chapters in a sequence other than presented.

The following are the chapter titles and page numbers to assist you with completing your personal navigation of this book.

Suggested Chapter Reflection & Reaction

I would suggest that prior to jumping into whichever chapter meets your needs that you give pause for a moment to reflect on the following and make some notes:

- Does this have applicability for me?

- What can I adopt from what I have read here?

- What are my potential needs for adaptation?

- What other issues do I see that I will need to address before embracing?

Please make note of your thoughts before proceeding.

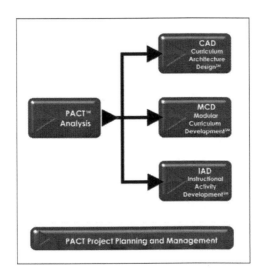

3 levels of ISD Methodologies
with common Analysis and
Project Planning & Management Methodologies.

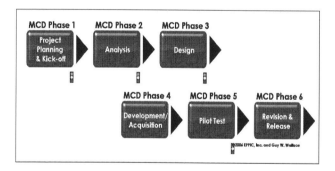

17 – BOOK SUMMARY AND CLOSE

Chapter Overview

This chapter is intended to summarize and close this book.

Book Summary

We have covered a lot in this book, including:

- MCD as an ADDIE-*like* methodology to conduct analysis, design and development of performance-based instructional and informational content for use during and/or before the moment of need
- The benefits of using these methods (adopted and/or adapted) for the Customers, the Suppliers and the Enterprise
- The Phases, Outputs, Teams and Tasks of an MCD effort at both an overview and at a detailed level
- The infrastructure and environmental supports required
- The key Knowledge and Skills required by the ISD Supplier Team members, especially the need to be a great facilitator of the Group Processes for analysis and design
- The uses, after extension, of the analysis data in support of other, non-instructional Enterprise systems and processes to work in unison with T&D/L&D to insure the Performance Competence of the people, the processes and the Enterprise

How you start is to just start.

Take the next project that comes up if it isn't something that should not be used as a learning and experimental effort. And use this book as your guide for planning and conducting an MCD effort.

All that remains before closing out this book is the next chapter with a few targeted readings as additional resources and references that align to the contents of this book.

Chapter Summary & Transition

This chapter was intended to summarize and close this book.

This chapter flows logically into the next, however your needs may cause you to want to skip around.

The following are the chapter titles and page numbers to assist you with any personal navigation needs.

Suggested Chapter Reflection & Reaction

I would suggest that prior to reviewing the final chapter of resources and references that you give pause for a moment to reflect on the following and make some notes:

- Does this have applicability for me?

- What can I adopt from what I have read here?

- What are my potential needs for adaptation?

- What other issues do I see that I will need to address before embracing?

Please make note of your thoughts before proceeding.

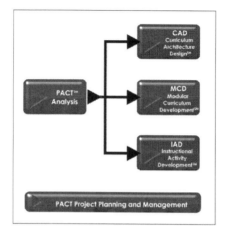

3 levels of ISD Methodologies
with common Analysis and
Project Planning & Management Methodologies.

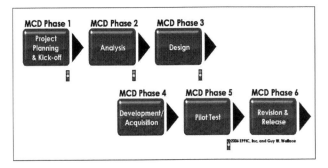

18 – ADDITIONAL RESOURCES & REFERENCES

Chapter Overview

This final chapter is intended to provide you with additional **Resources and References** to help you further with your analysis and post–analysis efforts.

These are not of general interest – that ocean is too large to boil down. These relate specifically to what has been covered in this book.

Resources and References

Books

Improving Performance: How to manage the white space on the organization chart. (1990) by Geary A. Rummler and Alan Brache

The late Dr. Rummler was a friend and a mentor, going back to 1980. I had the pleasure of working with him on a half dozen or so projects when I was at Motorola 1981–1982 – and in interacting with him on Client projects in the late 1990s and early 2000s. We also worked together in an attempt to clarify Human Performance Technology for our professional society back in 2003-2004.

My methods and the data I suggest capturing are actually derivatives of derivatives of his work when he co-led The Praxis Corporation in the 1970s with Tom Gilbert – which I learned in 1979. Any fault with these methods is attributed to me and certainly not to him.

The Quality RoadMap. (1994) by Ray Svenson, Karen Kennedy and Guy Wallace

This book is now out of print – but available at times as a used book. It presents a Business Architecture that we, the partners at SWI – Svenson & Wallace Inc. had developed and evolved and used in our consulting practices going back 10 years earlier. The book reflects our processes, practices and methods as used on a project with the Council for Continuous Improvement in the early 1990s.

Lean–ISD (1999) by Guy W. Wallace

ISD is an acronym for Instructional Systems Design. This book is available as a hardbound, a Kindle and as a free 404-page PDF at www.eppic.biz. It covers the analysis of the enabling Knowledge and Skills in great detail and the down-steam applications of that data in Curriculum Architecture Design efforts as well as in Content development efforts.

This book was the recipient of an Award of Excellence from the International Society for Performance Improvement in 2002.

L&D Systems View (2001) by Guy W. Wallace

This book is available as a hardbound, a Kindle and as a free PDF at www.eppic.biz. It covers the enabling Human and Environmental Assets as needed in a Learning & Development or Learning & Development function/department.

Management Areas of Performance (2007) BY Guy W. Wallace

This book is available as a free PDF at www.eppic.biz. It covers the Management Areas of Performance Model as a diagnostic tool and planning tool for Management Development for one's self and one's management staff.

Employee Performance-based Qualification/ Certification Systems (2008) by Ray Svenson & Guy W. Wallace

This book is available as a free PDF at www.eppic.biz. It covers the development of Performance Tests using the kind of analysis data presented in the Analysis of Performance Competence Requirements book.

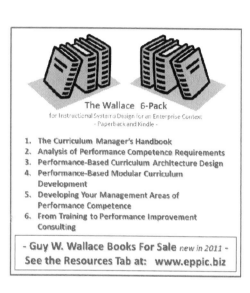

The Wallace 6-Pack
for Instructional Systems Design for an Enterprise Context
- Paperback and Kindle -

1. The Curriculum Manager's Handbook
2. Analysis of Performance Competence Requirements
3. Performance-Based Curriculum Architecture Design
4. Performance-Based Modular Curriculum Development
5. Developing Your Management Areas of Performance Competence
6. From Training to Performance Improvement Consulting

- Guy W. Wallace Books For Sale *new in 2011* -
See the Resources Tab at: www.eppic.biz

Handbook of Human Performance Technology 3rd Edition (2006) - Chapter 11: Modeling Mastery Performance and Systematically Deriving the Enablers for Performance Improvement by Guy W. Wallace. This chapter covers the basics of modeling performance and deriving the enablers.

Article

The following Article relates directly to the content of this book.

The Customer is King...Not! : Balancing Conflicting Stakeholder Requirements

Copyright: 1995, AQP - Author: Wallace, Guy W. - Journal for Quality and Participation, Vol. 18, No. 2, March 1995, pp. 84-89. This article articulates the various Stakeholder groups and presents a Stakeholder Requirements Matrices development instructions and an example.

Newsletter Articles

The following are a few of relevant Newsletter articles from over 10 years of publications – all available at www.eppic.biz – in the Resources Tab. Search them all using the titles here - or key words and phrases from this book.

Wallace, G.W. (2000) **The AoP Framework for Management**. Lean–ISD Newsletter, (3)1, 1,7. CADDI: Naperville: CADDI Inc.

Wallace, G.W. (2000) **L&D Systems View– 10 and 11 O' Clock.** Lean–ISD Newsletter, (3)4, 19–22. CADDI: Naperville: CADDI Inc.

Wallace, G.W. (2000) **Human Asset Management Planning & Management.** Lean–ISD Newsletter, (3)4, 27–27. CADDI: Naperville: CADDI Inc.

Wallace, G.W. (2000) **Environmental Asset Management Planning & Management**. Lean–ISD Newsletter (3)5, 43–43. CADDI: Naperville: CADDI Inc.

This chapter ends the book.

Your needs may have caused you to skip around the chapters in some other sequence that that presented.

The following are the chapters and page numbers for your personal navigation completion efforts.

Suggested Chapter Reflection & Reaction

I would suggest that prior to putting this book away – close by for future reference – that you give pause for a moment to reflect on the following and make some notes:

- Does this have applicability for me?

- What can I adopt from what I have read here?

- What are my potential needs for adaptation?

• What other issues do I see that I will need to address before embracing?

Please make note of your thoughts.

Guy W. Wallace

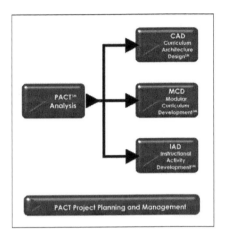

3 levels of ISD Methodologies
with common Analysis and
Project Planning & Management Methodologies.

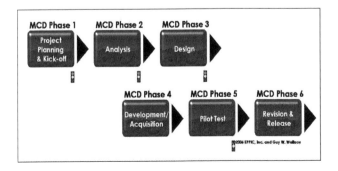

ABOUT THE AUTHOR

Guy W. Wallace has been in the performance improvement field since 1979 and has been an external consultant to government and industry since 1982. His Clients since then have include over 60 firms, with over 40 Fortune 500 firms; plus he has worked with NASA, NAVSEA, NAVAIR, NSA, BP, Opel, Siemen's Building Technologies.

He has analyzed, designed, and developed improvement interventions, including job and organizational designs, recruiting and selection systems, training and development, pay–for–performance systems for a wide variety of industries and business functions and Processes.

He is the author/ co–author of 8 books, several chapters, and more than 90 published articles beginning in 1984. Since 1982 he has presented more than 90 times at international conferences and local chapters of the International Society for Performance Improvement (ISPI), the American Society for Training & Development (ASTD), plus he has spoken at Training Magazine's Lakewood Conferences, the Association for Behavior Analysis (ABA), and the Conference on Nuclear Training & Education.

Guy W. Wallace served on the ISPI's executive committee as the treasurer for the 1999–2001 boards and as ISPI's president–elect and then president for 2002–2004.

He received ISPI's highest honorary award, the Honorary Member for Life Award for his contributions to both the Society and to the technology of Human Performance Technology (HPT) in 2010. His professional biography was listed in Who's Who in America in 2001 and he was designated a Certified Performance Technologist in 2002.

He was also recruited as an inaugural member of the American Society for Quality's (ASQ) Influential Voices campaign in 2010.

Guy's consulting Clients between 1982–2010 – and the number of engagements he performed for each Client is presented next.

Abbott Laboratories (3) – ALCOA (2) – ALCOA Labs (2) –
Alyeska Pipeline Services Company (2) – American Management
Systems (1) – Ameritech (1) – Amoco Corporation (13) – Arthur
Andersen (1) – ARCO of Alaska (3) – AT&T (4) – AT&T
Communications (1) – AT&T Microelectronics (1) – AT&T
Network Systems (24)

Bandag (7) – Bank of America (2) – Baxter (1) – Bellcore Tech (1)
– British Petroleum–America (1) – Burroughs (1) – Channel Gas
Industries/ Tenneco (1) – Commerce Clearing House (1) – Data
General (1) – Detroit Ball Bearing (1) – Digital Equipment
Corporation (2) – Discover Card (1) – Dow Chemical (3) – EDS
(1) – Eli Lilly (7) – Exxon Exploration (2)

Fireman's Fund Insurance (1) – Ford Design Institute (1) – Ford
Motor Company (1) – General Dynamics (10) – General Motors
(25) – GTE (1) – H&R Block (1) – Hewlett Packard (5) – Illinois
Bell (3) – Imperial Bondware (1) – Imperial Oil (1) – Johnson
Controls (1) – Kodak (1) – Lockheed (1) – MCC Powers (16) –
Motorola (1) – Multigraphics (1)

NASA (1) – NASCO (1) – NAVAIR (1) – NAVSEA (2) – NCR
(2) – Norfolk Naval Shipyard (4) – Northern Telecom (1) –
Northern Trust Bank (1) – NOVA (2) – Novacor (1) – Opel (1) –
Occidental Petroleum Labs (1) – Pacific Gas & Electric (1) –
Quaker (1) – Siemens Building Technologies (1) – Spartan Stores
(1) – Sphinx Pharmaceuticals (1) – Square D Company (2) –
SunTrust Banks (2) – Valuemetrics (1) – Verizon (3) – Verizon
Information Services (1) – Wells Fargo Advisors (1) –
Westinghouse Defense Electronics (1)

Overviews for each of the projects above may be found on his
web site at: www.eppic.biz

LinkedIn Reference

Richard E. Clark, PhD – USC
Professor and Director, Center for Cognitive Technology,
University of Southern California – clark@usc.edu

Dick Clark's LinkedIn Recommendation for Guy:
"My university research center concentrates on R&D in
evidence–based performance improvement and one of our
goals is to keep track of the activities of top professionals.
Guy Wallace constantly appears on our radar as the best
current example of the consummate professional in our field.
His broad experience, constant creativity, successful work
for his Clients and his original contributions to our field all
sum together into a very impressive career.

Guy has been working in the same field for a quarter century
and he could easily rest on his past accomplishments. Yet he
continues to create novel and exciting solutions for his
Clients. He invests considerable effort and so understands
both best practice and the huge body of research and
evaluation that supports practice.

He also spends quality time helping younger colleagues
develop and works to advance our profession though
professional organizations such as the International Society
for Performance Improvement (where he was elected
President a few years back) and the American Society for
Training and Development.

But what impresses me most about Guy is his ability to think
clearly about very complex problems. He has an exceptional
talent for stepping back from complex issues and generating
simple solutions and insights that are both sensible and
effective."

– Dick Clark – June 27, 2009

Guy W. Wallace

Details of Guy's background, accomplishments, education and experiences on over 250 Client projects may be found at his web site at:

www.eppic.biz

Guy has been offering formal workshops and less formal coaching sessions on the methods presented in this book since 1984. His Clients for these awareness, Knowledge and Skills development efforts include: Amoco, AT&T, Dow Chemical, Discover Card, EDS, Eli Lilly, General Motors, HP, MCC Powers (later Siemens Building Technologies), the Norfolk Naval Shipyard, NAVSEA, NASCO, NCR and SunTrust.

The Wallace 6-Pack

for Instructional Systems Design for an Enterprise Context
- Paperback and Kindle -

1. The Curriculum Manager's Handbook
2. Analysis of Performance Competence Requirements
3. Performance-Based Curriculum Architecture Design
4. Performance-Based Modular Curriculum Development
5. Developing Your Management Areas of Performance Competence
6. From Training to Performance Improvement Consulting

- Guy W. Wallace Books For Sale *new in 2011* -
See the Resources Tab at: www.eppic.biz

Made in the USA
Lexington, KY
17 April 2013